Changing Indian Society

Changing Indian Society

YOGESH ATAL

RAWAT PUBLICATIONS

Jaipur • New Delhi • Bangalore • Hyderabad • Guwahati

ISBN 978-81-316-0034-4 (HB)

Reprinted, 2024

Published by
Prem Rawat for **Rawat Publications**
Satyam Apts., Sector 3, Jawahar Nagar, Jaipur - 302 004 (India)
Phone: 0141 265 1748 / 7006 E-mail : info@rawatbooks.com
Website: rawatbooks.com

New Delhi Office
4858/24, Ansari Road, Daryaganj, New Delhi 110 002
Phone: 011-23263290

Also at *Bangalore, Guwahati* and *Kolkata*

Typeset by Rawat Computers, Jaipur
Printed at Nice Printing Press, New Delhi

Contents

Preface

When I began my career in the 1960s I made a commitment to do a book on Indian society that could serve as an introduction to the complex culture of India in sociological terms, and in a style intelligible to a non-specialist. That commitment is now fulfilled with the publication of this small book on the great country.

Even in the 1960s, there was no dearth of books on India written both by the insiders and the outsiders. The insiders profiled the society in Indological terms, as if Indian society was a Hindu society guided by the norms and prescriptions of the ancient sages, and has remained unchanged despite centuries of contact with the wider world. The outsiders were interested in the Indian exotica; representing underdevelopment on all fronts, India was treated as the house of all sorts of social evils. Flamed by the freedom struggle, some alleged pioneers of Indian sociology took cudgels with the foreign writers and blamed them for not understanding the basics of Indian society. By now, we all know the merits and demerits of research done by the insiders and the outsiders. Both bring in their respective biases. Generally, the insiders attempt to highlight the brighter side of the picture, and hide the so-called bad points; the outsiders, on the other hand, aim their eye on the dark side of the picture. It is the training in social scientific research that helps to a certain extent in erasing biases and ensuring objectivity. But the biases nevertheless remain, more so in the case of those who are ideologically committed.

In the 1960s a group of scholars pleaded for a "Sociology for India". They were again divided, foreign scholars (such as Louis Dumont) advocating for it had a stance different than the indigenous sociologists (such as A.K. Saran and R.N. Saksena). There was also a divide between social anthropologists and sociologists, each claiming independent boundaries for their respective disciplines. Those who refuted such claims and engaged themselves in empirical research finally won the race. Knowledge about Indian society today can be drawn from the works of such scholars who engaged in field research to document the *present* of India. A living society cannot be the replica of its past, howsoever glorious it might have been. People living its culture are not only carriers of tradition, but also its modernisers. India's present should certainly be seen in the backdrop of its long past that presents a veritable history of arrivals of, and encounters with, groups coming from abroad, and their subsequent assimilation into the multicultural fabric of India. But, the backdrop should not overwhelm the emerging structure of the society. Even the present would become part of the backdrop of India of the coming decades and centuries. This is its strength, its vitality.

The last four-five decades have witnessed enormous growth of empirical research in India, carried out in villages and cities, and on different problems in different parts of the country. There have also been efforts to conceptualise Indian reality in sociological terms. The picture of India that emerges from the findings of these various micro-studies – ethnographic and sample survey-based exercises – is vastly different from the earlier presentations. As against the "book view" and the "upper caste view" – to borrow the characterization given by Professor M.N. Srinivas – Indian society can be objectively portrayed on the basis of empirical evidence – both quantitative and qualitative.

As teacher and researcher of Indian society I can modestly claim my familiarity with this literature. Using the years of experience, and knowing the needs of students and others interested in getting introduced to this society, I have attempted to condense the vast storehouse of information in this simply written introduction to Indian society.

No doubt, each of the chapters in this book can be a subject matter of a full-scale opus. But this book carries only capsule summaries. Quite naturally, I had to be selective. There was no scope for me to go into the minutiae of each aspect of our society. I have also not dwelt on unending controversies, and have not propagated any ideological position. I have attempted to describe the structure of Indian society in the manner of a sociologist, and provided enough hints for further readings and research to those who wish to go deeper. For example, I have an abiding interest in caste – the subject on which I did my first research and published. But this book carries a small chapter on *Varna* and *Jati*, which is sufficient to provide a sociological orientation to the subject. Each chapter in this book is an introduction, a gateway to enter, not a final destination.

I began writing this text for the students of the 10+2 grade, but for some reasons I decided to abandon the effort. However, friends and colleagues who saw the drafts of those chapters convinced me of the utility of such an exercise and suggested that I complete this work keeping in view the audience consisting of (i) students doing their BA in social sciences, (ii) those preparing for some competitive examinations, such as the IAS, (iii) school teachers teaching sociology to higher secondary students, and (iv) the general public, including the foreign visitors interested in knowing about the structure of Indian society in a nutshell. Accordingly, I upgraded the chapters previously written, and maintained that standard for the new chapters.

The exercise that began in 2003 has now finished, thanks to the persuasion by Mr Kailash Rawat and his son Pranit of Rawat Publications. Without their continuous prodding, the unfinished manuscript would have remained in my files.

While writing the chapters, I invited some teenagers waiting to enter the eleventh standard to read the chapters and offer their comments, including the difficulties they found in any of the passages. I was indeed reassured when they complimented me for the "lucidity of my style". In this regard, I particularly wish to mention Nayantara Gupta and Sakshe Bhatt. Among the colleagues, who appreciated my effort and encouraged me to pursue, I would include Professor Surendra K. Gupta (previously of Panjabi University, Patiala) and Professor Rajesh Mishra and Dr Sukant Chaudhary (Lucknow University). I am also thankful to the students of the Birla Institute of Management Technology, New Delhi, whom I taught for a semester using the drafts of some of the chapters for a few lectures; some of their suggestions have also been incorporated in the revised text. I am also thankful to Dr Vivek Misra (Rani Durgawati University, Jabalpur), Dr Sunil Kumar (Shyamlal College, Delhi University), Dr Sangeet Ragi (Maharaj Agrasen College, Delhi University), and Dr Harish Sharma (Indian Council of Social Science Research) for their helpful comments on some of the chapters, particularly on Indian polity.

A book such as this will always have scope for improvement, and for additions. Suggestions, criticisms, and comments received from its readers will greatly help me in preparing its subsequent editions.

Yogesh Atal

1

India: Unity in Diversity

In this chapter . . .

India is a land of diversities woven together as a complex culture. It has been characterized as an indigenous civilization.

The country is second only to China in terms of its population size. In geographical spread, it is seventh in the world. It measures 3,214 km from North to South between latitudes 8°4' and 37°6' North, and 2,933 km from East to West between longitudes 68° 7' and 97°25' East. The mainland covers an area of 3.28 million sq km. Such a vast territory is rightly called a subcontinent as it juts away from the Asian mainland into the Indian Ocean. Bounded by the Himalayas in the North, stretching southward, it forms a peninsula surrounded by the Arabian Sea in the West, the Bay of Bengal in the East, and the Indian Ocean in the South.

A country of such a distinct geographical identity and vastness is characterized by varied topography and different climatic conditions. The Himalayan ranges separate the country from its Northern neighbours, namely Nepal, China, Bangladesh, and Bhutan. The Eastern mountain ranges demarcate its boundary with Myanmar, formerly known as Burma. In the North-West, India has a common border with Afghanistan and Pakistan. The Palk Strait and the Gulf of Mannar separate Sri Lanka from India. The archipelago state of the Maldives is also a close neighbour. The Indian territory also covers Lakshadweep (earlier known as the Laccadiv and Minicoy Islands) in the Arabian Sea and the Andaman and Nicobar Islands in the Bay of Bengal. India has a land frontier of about 15,200 km and a coastline, including those of its islands, of 7,516.6 km. Of India's land frontier, the longest stretch is the border with China – roughly 3,800 km from West to East, across difficult mountain ranges.

Indian society got redefined in August 1947, when the country attained its freedom from British colonial rule. It was also partitioned then with the creation of Pakistan, with a wing each in the Western and Eastern parts, separated from each other by nearly 1,600 km of intervening Indian corridor. Now, the two wings are the are two independent nations of Pakistan and Bangladesh. The Indian frontiers with these two countries are over 4,000 km.

While Pakistan was carved out through partition and created on the basis of religion, namely, Islam, what remained of India after the partition was a continuation of a multi-religious and multi-cultural pattern of social organization. The partition of the country not only changed its geographical boundaries, it also significantly affected its demography. It brought in a large refugee population from across the borders. The country also lost some of its population to Pakistan. However, India remained a unity composed of diversities. Even after the partition, Muslims constituted around 11 per cent of the country's population, more than the size of the population of the then West Pakistan. As against the Islamic Pakistan, India chose to be a Secular, Democratic Republic. The adjective, 'secular', was to emphasize the fact that no particular religious community dominated the country's polity.

Undivided India, bounded by mountains and seas, appeared to be a natural geographical unit. The Himalayas are like a vast wall of over 2,400 km, with several peaks. It is through the hazardous passes penetrating these mountains that waves of people from different lands arrived in the country.

The Himalayas also influence the climate of the country. They provide India with its principal river systems, and act as barrier checks to the South-West monsoon, thereby conserving the major part of the rain for the country. In addition, they halt the march of the icy winds coming down from the Arctic, across Siberia and Central Asia.

The rivers emanating from the Himalayas provided the highways of navigation and commerce in ancient times. They linked major cities and ports. The river banks offered sites for the cities, and water for irrigation to sustain agriculture in the rural areas. While the Ganga and Yamuna are regarded as holy rivers, there is a special place for the river Indus in Indian history. The river flows out of the Himalayas and pours into the Arabian Sea in the West. Its five tributaries – Jhelum, Chenab, Ravi, Beas, and Sutlej – gave Punjab its Persian name, the land of five (*panj*) rivers (*aab*). The Vedic Aryans called this river Sindhu (which, incidentally, also means sea in Sanskrit). The Persian speaking Iranians pronounced it as *Hindu*. The Greeks pronounced it as Indos and the Romans modified it to Indus. This name has stuck and the country's name – India – is derived from it. Its Persian name was Hindustan, again derived from the name of the river rather than from the Hindu religion. Most of the river Indus now flows in Pakistan, and the province named after it, Sindh, is also located there, but both India and Hindustan remain the names of the mainland. The Constitution of India calls the country 'India, that is, Bharat'.

The geography of the various regions has influenced the ways of life of the people living in them. The economy, habitat, and settlements, dress patterns, food habits, and language of each region are, to an extent, affected by the ecology of the area. Constant arrivals of people from other areas added further to the diversity in terms of race, language, religion, and material culture. Thus, various factors have contributed to the cultural diversity of India and to its rich cultural heritage.

The Rich Diversity of India

Plurality and multiplicity characterize Indian society and culture. India has accommodated and assimilated various outside elements into its growing culture. However, it has never been a 'melting pot' in which all differences got dissolved and a uniform identity was created. India is a shining example of a 'salad bowl' in which different elements retain their individual identities and yet, together, they form a distinct recipe. It is in that sense that India is a unity in diversity, guided by the principle of tolerance (*Sahishnuta*) and mutual respect.

Any living society is a product of its past. Through changes that occur internally, or are brought about by outside factors, societies continually redefine themselves. Through these processes, societies change in their demography, in their material culture, in their values, norms, and traditions, and in the patterns of behaviour of their members. Just as a newborn develops into a young, then an adult, and even later into an old person, so also does society grow. And just as a person continues to maintain his/her identity despite radical changes in his/her appearance, so also does a society maintain its identity in the midst of changes. In that sense, the Indian society of today is vastly different from what it was a hundred or a thousand years ago, and yet its composite culture is made up of the elements that it has retained from its past and the new elements that it has added from time to time. No living society is static. The pace of change may be slow or fast. When changes are slow in a society, it is termed a traditional society. But this does not mean that a traditional society is changeless. As one of the oldest civilizations, Indian society is a good example of continuity and change. Contemporary Indian society cannot be understood in terms of what is written in the *Shastras* and the *Smritis*. Our past provides a foundation on which the present is built, but it does not define the emerging contours of a living society.

Indian civilization is about 5,000 years old. It has a chequered history. This vast subcontinent has seen several waves of migration. Groups of people coming from different corners of the world with different intentions confronted the local populace and were finally accepted. Each such interaction resulted in give and take between the host community and the arriving migrants. Their differences and the intermingling of traits continually changed the living culture of the people and enriched the growing Indian civilization. Historians seem to be of the view that people called Aryans inhabited the Indus river valley almost 2,500 years before the birth of Christ. Since they belonged to the same racial stock and spoke the same language, the term, Aryan, was used to distinguish them from the relatively dark-skinned people speaking Dravidian languages. Ethnically, the Aryans represented the Caucasoid and the Dravidians the Proto-Australoid races.[1]

The Aryans overwhelmed Northern India, while the Dravidians moved South. Deriving from the river Indus, also called the Sindhu, the evolving religion of the area came to be known as Hindu, which built on the *Vedas* of the Aryans and gradually assimilated many local cults and traditions. Buddhism began as a protest against the rigidities occurring within Hinduism somewhere around 500 BC and soon spread to other Asian lands. The Greeks, under Alexander the Great, invaded the country in 327 BC, but they were soon driven out. Chandragupta Maurya was the first Indian ruler who succeeded in extending his empire across the whole of North India with its capital at the present site of Patna (then known as Patliputra), the capital of Bihar. The Maurya Empire reached its peak during the reign of Ashok, the grandson of Chandragupta Maurya, who ruled from 273 to 232 BC. He converted to Buddhism and sent his emissaries to distant lands to spread the new religion. But in another hundred years, the Mauryas lost their hold when other empires rose and fell. The Sunga dynasty was one of these that ruled for a hundred years. This dynasty brought back Hinduism, replacing Buddhism. In 320 AD, another ruler named Chandra Gupta founded the Gupta dynasty, which lasted for 160 years. The Huns, who entered Indian territory around 450 AD, defeated the Guptas. The Gupta period is described as the Golden Age of India because it was during this time that both arts and sciences flourished in the country. The famous Sanskrit poet, Kalidas, lived during this period.

By the end of the 5th Century AD, Northern India got divided into various Hindu kingdoms.

The Southern part of India remained relatively untouched by the mighty empires of the North. It was also divided into different kingdoms and had its own maritime trade relations with other countries such as Sri Lanka and Indonesia. However, spiritual and intellectual linkages got strengthened between the North and the South. Rishis and religious teachers took Vedic wisdom and the Sanskrit language to the South, and introduced there the Aryan gods and sacred rituals of their worship. In this exchange, Dravidian gods and goddesses, and the rituals associated with them, also passed into the Aryan stream. The two civilizations mingled and the present-day Hindu can be regarded as a product of this fusion of cultures.

The situation changed with the arrival of Islam. The first entrants were traders who frequented the Western coast, mostly in Malabar. Their marriages with the local women resulted in new groups such as Moplah (in Malabar), Natia (in Konkan), and Labbais (on the East coast of Tamil Nadu). After the 8th century, there was a continuous inflow of Muslim traders and preachers, who visited different places and spread their religion. However, Sindh, which is now part of Pakistan, was invaded and conquered by the Arabs in 732 AD. Several raids were carried out by the troops of Mahmud Ghazni during 997-1030 AD. Muhammad Ghori defeated Delhi's king Prithviraj Chauhan, in 1192. Qutab-ud-Din Aibak established the Delhi Sultanate in 1206; that started the period of Muslim rule in most of Northern India. It may be mentioned that all of these invaders did not come from the same stock. The early rulers were Turkish and Afghan in origin, and they were later superseded by the Moghuls.

The first Europeans arrived in the country in the 15th century. Portuguese sailor Vasco da Gama landed in Kozhikode in Kerala in 1498. The Portuguese took possession of Goa in 1510. The British East India Company arrived in 1613 and established itself on the Eastern coast. Started as a business company, this organization began spreading its hold and even fought a battle with the local Muslim rulers in Plassey in 1757. Kolkata thus became the centre of British power. After the Indian mutiny of 1857, the East India Company handed over control to the British Crown. The British set up an empire that consisted of British India and a patchwork of native states owing allegiance to the British Crown. The empire covered present-day Pakistan and Bangladesh and Myanmar (known then as Burma).

Towards the end of the 19th century, nationalist opposition to British rule became quite prominent. This was consolidated and made more forceful under the leadership of Mahatma Gandhi.

India finally got its independence from the British on 15 August 1947, but it was divided into two states, India and Pakistan. The divided Pakistan had two wings, one in the West comprising Western Punjab, Sindh, and Baluchistan, and the other in the East, taking away the Eastern part of Bengal from India. The partition was caused by the two-nation theory propounded by the advocates of Pakistan. They argued that the Muslims were a separate nation and, therefore, should have a separate homeland. Thus, the areas that went to Pakistan were those that had a preponderance of Muslims. This resulted in the uprooting of several Hindu families from the areas that went to Pakistan. But the partition did not change the multi-religious composition of India, as only a small percentage of Muslims from the rest of India opted to move to Pakistan; most of them decided to stay on in India.

Racial Profile

Biologically, all human beings belong to a single genus and species called *Homo Sapiens*. However, population groups living together in different parts of the world show some physical characteristics that distinguish them from other groups. Such biologically distinguished groups are called races. The characteristics that help identify different racial groups include colour and texture of hair, quantity and distribution of hair on the body, colour of the eyes, shape of the eyelids, shape of the nose, the lips, and the skull, skin colour, and body height. Since in early times, people with the same racial features stayed together, spoke the same language, and lived the same culture, race was mistakenly used as a synonym for language, culture, religion, and a society. It is a fallacy to think of one race as belonging to one culture. Race is a biological concept. It is wrong to associate race with intelligence, or regard any race as superior or inferior to others.

Societies such as India that are spread in a vast area of geographical diversities have been home to several races and have received several migrant groups from abroad over a course of thousands of years. This has made India a multi-racial country. Moreover, through intermarriages between people of different races, a good deal of miscegenation has occurred. Pure races are now only theoretical constructs. This is true of India as well.

However, it will be useful to have an idea of the racial profile of India.

There is very little fossil evidence of the prehistoric times to suggest the ethnic stocks of those who inhabited the vast subcontinent. All accounts of the Indus Valley civilization that prospered in Sindh and the Punjab, which are now part of Pakistan, indicate that people of mixed origins and diverse racial types lived there in those days. Waves of migrations from different corners of the world made this country home of diverse races. Intermarriages between people of different racial stocks have made the task of researchers rather difficult in fixing racial origins. During the Census operations of 1891, Sir Herbert Hope Risley attempted the first ever classification of the people of India into different racial types. He classified them into the following seven types: Turko-Iranian, Indo-Aryan, Scytho-Dravidian, Aryo-Dravidian, Mongolo-Dravidian, Mongoloid, and Dravidian. This classification was criticised by other scholars because Risley mixed linguistic categories (Aryan and Dravidian) with the racial categories. In earlier times, the racial boundaries might have coincided with linguistic boundaries, but technically, language is a learnt behaviour and is not biologically transmitted. Egon von Eickstedt propounded the theory that South India had a Proto-Negroid population long before the other racial stocks arrived. During the 1931 Census, B.S. Guha took anthropometric measurements in different parts of the country to determine the physical characteristics of different groups and identified six main races with nine subtypes. That classification is still being used, though the exact size of these groups in Indian society cannot be determined. However, this classification is good evidence that the people of India are composed of various racial types, making it a multi-racial country. Guha's classification is as given below:

1. The Negrito
2. The Proto-Australoid
3. The Mongoloid:
    - (i) Palaeo-Mongoloid
        - (a) Long-headed (Dolichocephalic)*
        - (b) Broad-headed (Brachycephalic)*
    - (ii) Tibeto-Mongoloid
4. The Mediterranean:
    - (i) Palaeo-Mediterranean
    - (ii) Mediterranean
    - (iii) Oriental
5. The Western Brachycephals:
    - (i) Alpinoid
    - (ii) Dinaric
    - (iii) Armenoid
6. The Nordic

Many scholars have disputed the existence of Negrito strain in the Indian population. Most anthropologists agree that the earliest known inhabitants of India were probably proto-Australoids, who may have received some infiltration of Negrito. The only point that we can mention with certainty is that Indian population is composed of various racial strains. Representatives of all the three major races of the world, namely Caucasoid, Mongoloid, and Negroid, are found in this country. Since there

---

* Anthropologists compute a Cephalic Index (the word cephal derived from Greek, meaning 'head') to classify heads into long or broad or medium. The Cephalic Index is the ratio of the greatest breadth of the human head to its greatest length, from front to back, multiplied by 100. When the width of the head is less than 76 per cent of its length from front to back, it is called Dolichocephalic; when the width is 81 per cent or more of its length, it is called Brachycephalic. The intermediate head shape, with a width of 76 to 80.9 per cent of its length, is called Mesocephalic. The same index used for skulls is called the Cranial Index, and the types are described as Dolichocranial, Brachycranial, and Mesocranial.

has been so much miscegenation, no race exits in its pure form and detailed subclassification and calculation of the size of each group is almost impossible.

India's population includes more than 400 tribal groups spread in different parts of the country, but largely concentrated in Central India and in the Northeast region. According to the 1991 Census, the combined population of these groups constituted 8.08 per cent of the total population of India. Besides these tribal communities, the Hindu population is divided into a large number of castes. Since the enumeration of castes in the Census was discontinued in 1931, we do not have the exact numbers of these castes, but various estimates suggest that there are more than 3,000 castes within the Hindu fold. Both the tribes and castes are also called ethnic groups. An ethnic group is said to share common racial characteristics, share a common territory, practise the same religion, and it is an in-marrying group (which is technically called endogamous). The division of society into ethnic groups makes India a heterogeneous society.

Linguistic Diversity

India is rightly described as a polyglot country – a country of many languages. Linguistic research suggests that when means of transportation were less developed, there was little mobility of people. Therefore, communities confined to small areas spoke their own dialects. And these were spoken in a radius of 7-8 kilometres. That is why even today there are 1,572 languages and dialects that are each spoken by less than 1,00,000 speakers, besides the 18 Scheduled languages. Until recently, the Census of India collected only mother tongue statistics, which gave the wrong impression about the actual number of speakers of any language. The fact of the matter is that many people speak more than one language; there are also instances of people who do not speak their mother tongue, but speak other languages of the region in which they have settled. However, it is important to note that there is no state in the Indian Union that is monolingual in terms of mother tongue. And, in most of the states, Hindi figures among the top three languages returned as a mother tongue. The 1991 Census mentions Hindi as the most prominent mother tongue, spoken by 39.85 per cent of people; if we add Urdu to it, which uses a different script, but the same grammar, and is, therefore, commonly understood, the percentage will go up to 44.98. Certainly, the number of speakers of this language is much greater than this percentage, which consists only of those who reported Hindi or Urdu as their mother tongue.

The comparative strength of scheduled languages, in terms of those returning them as mother tongue is shown in Table 1.

Table 1
Mother Tongue Statistics 1991

	Language	*Persons who Returned the Language as Their Mother Tongue*	*Percentage to Total Population*
1.	Hindi	33,72,72,114	39.85
2.	Bengali	6,95,95,738	8.22
3.	Telugu	6,60,17,615	7.80
4.	Marathi	6,24,81,681	7.38
5.	Tamil	5,30,06,368	6.26
6.	Urdu	4,3406,932	5.13
7.	Gujarati	4,06,73,814	4.81
8.	Kannada	3,27,53,676	3.87
9.	Malayalam	3,03,77,176	3.59
10.	Oriya	2,80,61,313	3.32
11.	Punjabi	2,33,78,744	2.76
12.	Assamese	1,30,79,696	1.55
13.	Sindhi	21,22,848	0.25
14.	Nepali	20,76,645	0.25
15.	Konkani	17,60,607	0.21
16.	Manipuri	12,70,216	0.15
17.	Kashmiri	38,79,584	0.46
18.	Sanskrit	49,736	0.01

The table shows that barring Sanskrit, which is reported to be the mother tongue of less than 50,000 people, each of the remaining 17 languages is spoken by more than a million people, with Manipuri spoken by 1.27 million people and Hindi by 337 million people, according to the 1991 Census. If we assume the same percentage of people reporting Hindi as the mother tongue in the recently held 2001 Census, then the figure will be as high as 410 million people. The table does not give the number of persons who regard English as their mother tongue. But we all know that most educated persons in India have a fair knowledge of English. An exact idea of India's linguistic profile can be had only when we have data about the number of languages spoken by each individual. Such a statistics will put the number of Hindi speaking persons much higher than the mother tongue statistics that we have presented in the above table. However, even these data reflect the great linguistic diversity of India. Moreover, each of these 18 languages has rich literature; there are also several Indian writers who have earned international fame by writing in English, not only fiction, but also on technical subjects.

It should be mentioned that linguistic diversity is found in each of the states of the Indian Union. It is true that after India got independence, the states were reorganised on the basis of language, but such reorganization did not erase the multilingual character of the individual states.

Plurality of Religions

Indian society is multi-religious. While the state is secular, the people of India belong to different religions. Apart from the tribal societies, many of whom still live in the pre-religious state of animism and magic, the Indian population consists of the Hindus (82.41%), Muslims (11.6%), Christians (2.32%), Sikhs (1.99%), Buddhists (0.77%) and Jains (0.41%).

The Hindus themselves are divided into several sects; in fact, Jainism, Sikhism, and Buddhism are all offshoots of the same

Places of worship

root. Hinduism is also said to have incorporated many practices and beliefs of the local communities. J.H. Hutton was of the view that the "tribal religions...represent, as it were, surplus material not yet built into the temple of Hinduism". This explains the nature of Hinduism, which is polytheistic, having several million gods and goddesses. Many local cults and parochial practices have been amalgamated and become part of the great tradition of Hinduism. Similarly, many of the universal traits and practices of Hinduism got localized, or have got differently interpreted in different regions. Mckim Marriott called these interactions between the Great Tradition and the several little traditions in the indigenous civilization of India as processes of 'universalization' and 'parochialization'.[2]

Practitioners of Hinduism are mainly divided between the *Vaishnavs* (worshippers of Vishnu), *Shaivaites* (worshippers of Shiva), *Shaktas* (worshipper of the mother goddess, Shakti), and *Smartas* (worshippers of all the three – Vishnu, Shiva, and Shakti). There are subdivisions in each of them. Similarly, there are several movements that are mistaken as separate religions such as Lingayat, Kabirpanth, Radhaswamy, Swami Narayani, Arya Samaj, and Brahmo Samaj. In that sense, Hinduism is not a monolithic whole. It allows its adherents to follow whatever path they choose to follow for worship. It is this catholicity that makes Hinduism not a religion in the sense in which it is used for other religions. It is a way of life, and allows for diversity.

Although Buddhism, Jainism, and Sikhism are counted as separate religions, they originated as protest movements against the caste system of the Hindus. But these religions have not been able to eliminate casteism. For example, the lower castes among the Sikhs are called *Majhabis*, and in their villages, they are never addressed as 'Sardar'. However, no untouchability is observed in gurudwaras. Research has shown that occupational castes still maintain their separate identity among the Sikhs and marriages generally take place along caste lines. The same is true among the

Jains, who are not only divided into different sects such as *Digambars* (without clothes) and *Shwetambars* (with white robes), and into subsects such as *Barahpanthi* and *Terahpanthi*, but also into different castes. It is also interesting to note that the Jains have Brahman priests in their temples. The Brahman priests also conduct marriages among them. Similarly, wholesale conversion of castes into Buddhism has meant only change of religion without loss of caste identity. Even the converts continue to self-define themselves as Dalits.

The arrival of Islam in India added to the plurality of religions in the country. Interaction with the arriving religion also resulted in conversion to Islam, making the Muslim community diverse in terms of the migrant Muslims (called *Ashrafs*) and the converts (called *Azlafs*). Despite the conversion, the lower status of these caste groups continued in the new affiliation. Furthermore, the Muslims themselves are divided into the *Shia* and *Sunni* sects. There is also a group of people called the *Ahmedias*, the status of which has always caused tension in the Muslim community. It should be noted that there are four schools of Muslim Law – the Shafi School, Hanifi School, Mallki School, and Hanbali School. Within Islam, there are 14 religious orders, such as Chisti, Suhrawardi, Naqsbandi, Qadiri, etc. Diversity, thus, characterizes the Muslim community also.

Christianity was introduced in Kerala in the first century AD when the apostle, St. Thomas, landed there and converted many Namboodiripad Brahmans and others, and founded seven churches on the Malabar coast. These Converts and their descendants are called Syrian Christians. But not all present-day Indian Christians belong to this group. The Christians are also divided between Roman Catholics and Protestants. There are different denominational churches. It should also be noted that the converted Christians retained their separate identity. Thus, missionary activities in the tribal areas contributed to the spread of Christianity, but these groups remained tribal. So is the case with many Dalit groups who chose to convert to Christianity. As a result of mixed marriages between the British nationals and the local Indians, another group of Anglo-Indians got created among the Christians.

India also has small religious groups of Parsees and Jews. The Parsees arrived from Persia in the 8th century AD and settled on the Western coast. Practising Zoroastrianism, the Parsees speak Gujarati, and wear a distinct dress that bears the Indian imprint. What distinguishes them from the rest is the manner of their speaking Hindi and the rituals. As traders, they have assimilated themselves with the local community.

The Jews were concentrated in Kochi in Kerala and Konkan in Maharashtra. The Jews settled in Konkan were known as the Shanwar Teli because they were oil pressers and did not work on Saturdays (Shanivar). Now they are called Bene Israel. Most of these Jews are to be found in Mumbai and its surrounding areas. Some of them have gone back to Israel.

Threads of Unity

The indigenous civilization of India is a result of accommodation and amalgam of different peoples who came from different locations and made this country their final destination. To quote Gertrude Emerson Sen, from the book *Cultural Unity of India:*[3]

> In the thousand year period between 500 BC and AD 500, Persians, Greeks, Sakas, Kushans, and Huns all succeeded in forcing their way into India...They overran the North-West and either detached it from the rest of India by temporarily adding it to some empire of their own... or they set themselves up as local rulers in the Punjab,...or else, descending upon India as wanton looters...All such

> invasions were of a temporary nature, and their force was invariably spent in one, two, or three centuries at the most. In the end, practically all these foreigners had become so thoroughly Indianized, through intermarriage and adoption of Indian manners, languages, and customs that they had ceased to be foreigners. This was a tribute to the innate strength of Indian culture, as expressed in its basic ideas and institutions, but it was also a proof of the strangely flexible character of the Indian mind. India might not have resisted political conquest, but she soon made the conquerors her own by accepting them into her fold [p. 18].

From each of these immigrant groups, some elements were picked up and made part of the Indian way of life. The Mauryan Empire borrowed the administrative model of the Persian Empire. From the Greeks, India learnt the craft of minting coinage. The Kushans brought the famous Gandharan art, which was used for spreading Buddhism. Powerful Rajput clans are said to be the offsprings of the chieftains of the Saka and Hun tribes.

The geography of this vast subcontinent facilitated concentration of people in distinct regions. While adventurous persons migrated and settled in alien regions, difficulties of transportation generally discouraged mobility. That is how a number of regional regimes existed prior to the arrival of the Muslims and, later, the British. Both the Muslim rulers and the British made efforts to create a single political unity. But they could not erase regional differences and cultural diversities. In fact, every new arrival of outside groups, for purposes of trade, or spread of religion, or to annexe power, resulted in further addition to the diversities.

The diversities that we have mentioned at the national level are also to be found in each region. In every geographical region, we find people of different religions, with different racial features, and a mix of languages. In terms of dress, language, and food habits, each region shows its distinctive character and these similarities cut across religious and racial boundaries. Thus, the Muslims or Christians of Kerala have much more in common with other Keralites than with their co-religionists in Uttar Pradesh or Andhra Pradesh. In this sense, while the religion provides an inter-regional unity to its practitioners, a region binds people of different religions in a common bond of provincial culture.

From ancient times, there were several channels to link the various parts of the country. Important among these were the centres of higher learning – ashrams and universities such as Takshsila (also called Taxila, which is now in Pakistan). "In later centuries, Srinagar...took its place as the great northern seat of learning and pandits flocked thither from far and near. Sravasti, Kasi, Pataliputra, Nalanda, Vikramsila, Somapuri (Paharpur) and Tamluk were the famous centres of higher studies in what are now Uttar Pradesh, Bihar, and Bengal. Ujjain in Western Malwa, Padmavati near modern Gwalior, Vanavasi in the Konkan, and Vallabhi and Palitana in Saurashtra were the principal centres in Central and Western India. Andhra had its Amaravati and Nagarjunkonda. In South India, besides Madurai, there was Kanchi or Conjeevaram. During the period of Pallava supremacy, between the 4th and 19th centuries AD, Kanchi was the greatest university town of Southern India" (Sen, 1969: 32).

Another significant factor that helped disseminate a common culture was the visits of wandering storytellers to different communities. Through them, the stories of the great epics of the *Ramayana*, *Mahabharata*, and the *Puranas* reached the vast numbers of illiterate masses. These stories were also dramatized. In this manner, the great tradition of India reached millions of masses in different corners of India. In the process, many stories wore local parochial colours. Similarly, these wandering storytellers and minstrels picked up local stories of parochial heroes and events, and went on publicizing them to wider audiences adding literary flavour to them and linking them with some great traditional elements. Thus, many parochial themes became universal. These twin processes linked India's several little traditions with the great tradition of India. David Mandelbaum notes: "Travelling performers and sages have linked villagers to the artistic and religious centres for centuries, disseminating the ideas and precepts of the larger organization...In the 19th century, these ties were strengthened by improved travel, railways, postal services, and printed matter. More recently, the ties have been enhanced by cinema and radio."[4] With the arrival of TV and the introduction of several channels, this process has been further speeded up. The TV serials based on the lives of Ram and of Krishna – two major figures in Hindu mythology – have significantly contributed in the rejuvenation of tradition.

A common culture also spread through the arts. The temples of the Hindus, Buddhists, and Jains became the abodes of divine statues. The magnificent architecture of these temples and the iconography promoted through them helped develop a world of images commonly shared by the people of India. With the arrival of the printing press, the personified images of the myriad gods and goddesses reached a multitude of homes through calendars and posters. South India's city, Sivakasi, became the key centre for the production of such religious calendars. This gave rise to different schools of sculpture and of painting, which promoted the same themes and same divinities, but introduced local variations. Mughal architecture added further to the richness of India's culture. The various forts, tombs, minarets, and imperial gardens attracted, and still attract, visitors from all over the country. If people go to the temples of Khajuraho, or Konark, or Meenakshipuram, they also visit the Taj Mahal, Red Fort, and the Qutub Minar, the Buddhist temples of Sanchi and Sarnath, and the Jain temples of Mount Abu and Ranakpur. They are all part of India's proud cultural heritage.

During the period of regional regimes, when different Maharajas or Nawabs ruled, the country was politically divided into several principalities and kingdoms, but was tied together through a complicated network of cultural and religious linkages. Pilgrim centres located in different parts of the country attracted people from everywhere. For Hindus, the pilgrimage to four locations (The *Chaar Dhaam*) was, and still is, a major motivation to travel. These places are Badrinath in the Himalayas, Jagannath Puri in Orissa, Rameshwaram in Tamil Nadu, and Dwarka in Gujarat. Similarly, the Kumbha Mela (Pitcher Fair), held every fourth year at a different destination – Hardwar (in Uttaranchal), Allahabad (in Uttar Pradesh), Ujjain (in Madhya Pradesh), and Nashik (in Maharashtra) – collects lakhs of people from all over the country for a holy dip. In earlier times, it used to take months to complete a pilgrimage because of the poor infrastructure for travelling. During the British rule, a major change occurred when, in 1853, railways were introduced. Construction of roads and railway tracks greatly improved the mobility of people from one region to another.

The British greatly succeeded in creating a supra-regional structure of political administration. As one political unity, with a central authority, all the regions began to share a common political culture. We can briefly mention here some features of India's emerging common culture:*

1. *Emergence of an Elaborate Bureaucracy:* The British created an all-India civil service, then known as the ICS. In independent India, it was renamed the Indian Administrative Service (IAS). The country was provided with a common system of administration, and the administrators were recruited from all parts of India and from different groups. In independent India, the size of the bureaucracy has greatly enlarged and

---

* This is based on Yogesh Atal, *Building a Nation: Essays on India*, Chapter 14, titled "Communication and Nation Building in India". Abhinav Publications, New Delhi, 1981.

special provisions have been made to recruit people from the underprivileged groups, backward classes, scheduled castes, and tribes.

2. *Formation of a National Army:* A common army for the country as a whole was another indication of a unified nation. The British created regiments that highlighted the participation of special regions or communities, such as the Sikh Regiment, Gorkha Regiment, Jat Regiment, and Rajputana Rifles. Thus, the unified army reflected the diversity of India.
3. *Evolution of an Effective Communication Strategy:* The British introduced English as the language of administration. Its use in different regions helped break the linguistic barrier. They also introduced modern schooling to remove illiteracy and expose children to the wider world. The system of modern education also encouraged publishing in local and vernacular languages. Radio and newspapers reached individual homes and helped create and enlarge people's awareness about India and the world. The development of transportation and communication (publishing, telegraph, telephone, newspapers and magazines, and radio) played an important role in linking the various parts of the country and developing a sense of Indianness. These channels were also used for promoting traditional bonds and spreading traditional culture.
4. *Rise of Nationalism.* While the British brought about changes to ensure better administration, they also exposed people to Western ideas of nation, democracy, and freedom. Modern education created a middle class, and gave rise to a national leadership that united the people to fight against foreign rule. The freedom struggle served as a major unifying force. The leadership called all sections of society to join the struggle. People of different religions and of both sexes

> united to join the freedom movement. Nationalism rose above caste, religion, and region. Responding to the growing demand for 'Home Rule', the British gradually introduced democratic principles. This resulted in the formation of all-India political parties. The growing unity worried the British. To counter this, they adopted the policy of 'Divide and Rule'. They encouraged religious minorities to claim separate electorates. They also developed programmes and activities for the castes of the lower strata, calling them 'exterior' or 'depressed castes'. The call for a separate state for the Muslims, Pakistan, was a result of this policy, which finally succeeded in fracturing the unity of India.

The unity of India is manifest in several ways. First, the country is a political unity, called the Indian Union. It has a Constitution that was adopted on 26 January 1950. Elected representatives from different constituencies spread all over the country constitute its Parliament. There is a common judiciary, a common currency, and a free flow of its citizens from one part of the country to the other. All nationals carry a common passport. People of any given region are variously linked with other regions through religion, language, business, government, and politics.

India can rightly be called a multiplicity, or a plural society. Its complex culture is composed of five distinct elements: the local culture of little traditions; the regional culture; the classical cultures or great traditions associated with major religions such as Hinduism, Buddhism, Sikhism, Islam, Christianity, etc.; the emerging and growing national culture; and the elements of a global culture. There is a good mix of all these elements in the different regions. Years of exposure to the outside world and assimilation of immigrant groups into the cultural fabric of Indian society, have created this multiplicity. The assimilated traits have assumed new meanings and functions and, thus, they have become Indianized.

The Hindu-Sikh relationship is compared with the finger and the nail. As the nail cannot be separated from the finger without damage, so the Sikhs cannot be separated from the Hindus. It has been a tradition among Hindu families in the Punjab to offer one son to the Sikh religion. Thus, there are many families that have a mix of the Sikh and the *Mona*. "When Arjun, fifth in the line of Sikh gurus, collected the writings of earlier Gurus and compiled the *Adi-Granth* – the sacred book of the Sikhs – compiled in 1603-04, many devotional hymns of the Vaishnava saints were included. Poems of Namdev and Tukaram, of Ramananda, of Kabir, and his cobbler disciple, Ravidasa, all form part of the sacred *Granth*. But Kabir's Hindi stanzas, which are included, number more than a thousand, showing the great part he played in the early development of Sikhism in the Punjab, before the tenth and last Guru, Govind Singh, transformed the Sikhs into the militant community of the Khalsa at the end of the 17th century" (Sen, 1969: 51).

A story goes that when the Parsees came to India, their leader asked the hosts to bring a glass of milk and some sugar. He then mixed the two in the presence of everybody and remarked: "As the sugar dissolves in the milk and may impart sweetness to it, we shall mix in your society and the result will be sweet." The immigrant Parsees now form an integral part of Indian society.

The famous Urdu poet, Mohammed Iqbal, who later chose to side with Pakistan, wrote the famous song that is sung in India today: *Saare jahan se achcha Hindositan hamara, Hum bulbule hain uski woh gulsitan hamara* (Hindustan is the best in the world. It is our garden and we are its birds). In the same song, he preached: *Mazhab nahin sikhata hame aapas me bair rakhna* (Religion does not teach us to be each other's enemies). Songs written by the famous poet, Amir Khusro, a disciple of Hazrat Nizamuddin, are sung at weddings both among the Hindus and the Muslims in Northern India and even in Pakistan. Well-known

Nobel laureate Indian poet Rabindra Nath Tagore has authored the poems that have been adopted as the national anthems of both India and Bangladesh. As said earlier, the holy book of the Sikhs (*Guru Granth Sahib*) is an anthology of songs and bhajans, many of which were written by Hindu saints and poets.

Priests from Christian churches and Muslim mosques in Kerala participate in the Vijaya Dasami festival of the Hindus. They vie with each other to perform the Hindu ritual of *Vidyarambham* – initiation of children into the world of learning. On the 12th October 2005, Vijaya Dasami day, twelve children, including four girls, uttered the first letter of their life sitting in the lap of the Imam of the Cheraman Juma Masjid of Thiruvananthapuram.[5] Even churches participated in the ritual. The St George Orthodox Church in Thiruvananthapuram "conducted the ceremony for the third consecutive year by initiating 45 children belonging to different religions. Similarly, the Niranom Orthodox Syrian Church in Tiruvalla initiated over hundred children on this day." The Hindu ritual has assumed a secular – or a multi-religious character in the state of Kerala.

Hindi as a link language is spreading far and wide. Its integrative role cannot be denied. Rather than replacing other regional languages, Hindi is becoming an additional language that is spoken by millions. The mass media have played a vital role in this regard.

One also notices the emergence of a common cuisine with an all-India spread. Certain South Indian dishes like *dosa-idly-sambhar*, *Tandoori* dishes from the Punjab, the *dhoklas* of Gujarat, and the *sandesh* and *rasgulla* of Bengal are now part of an all-India cuisine. Confectioners like Haldiram are now known not only all over India, but also in a large number of countries to meet the demands of the Indian diaspora.

In matters of dress, too, women in all parts of India are now adopting the *salwar-kameez*, without giving up the traditional

Sari. Both men and women wear the jeans of the West with the khadi kurtas of India.

The emerging national culture of India has a queer mix of several elements from different subcultures and even cultural traits and complexes from abroad. And yet it remains distinctively Indian. Adoption of outside traits has not always been at the cost of the traditional. A mixed culture of diversities makes a judicious combination of the native and the alien, traditional and the modern, old and the new.

The challenges to national integration, however, remain. When a society is composed of so many diverse elements, and has such a long history, it is inevitable that there may arise conflicts of interest. Politics also encourages articulation of interests. In a democracy, the opposition parties are expected to criticize the government and even mobilize support to wrest power. All this leads to organization of interest groups along caste, communal, or ethnic lines. Regions get agitated over differential treatment. In the past, the country has faced several such movements and protests, including demands for separation. But these factors that threaten unity have been handled successfully. However, the solution of one conflict does not mean the end of all conflicts. New situations of conflict arise, and the society has to mobilize its resources to resolve them and to bring in a climate of cooperation. This is why sociologists call a society 'cooperation crossed by conflict'. India is no exception.

Notes

1. Technically, the term 'Aryan' is a linguistic category. It should not be confused with race.

2. See Mckim Mariott's essay titled 'Little Communities in an Indigenous Civilization', in the book edited by him, *Village India,* 1955, University of Chicago.
3. Sen, Gertrude Emerson, *Cultural Unity of India*, 1969, Publications Division, Ministry of Information and Broadcasting, Government of India, New Delhi.
4. See David G Mandelbaum, *Society in India,* 1972, Popular Prakashan, Mumbai, p. 387.
5. This mosque is claimed to be the first mosque in the country.

2

Population Profile

In this chapter . . .

For understanding any society, the first thing to know is the size of its membership, and its distribution in terms of sex, age, place of residence, and other socially significant characteristics, such as marital status, education, occupation, religious affiliation, etc. This is technically called demography.[1] Information about a given population on its demographic variables helps understand the way a society is structured and the problems that it has to address. All the subsystems of society – namely, polity, economy, social organization, and culture – are affected by a society's demography.

Like any social group, a society is composed of people. Its membership is recruited either through sexual reproduction within it, or through in-migration of individuals or groups from other societies. Similarly, it loses its members when they die out or migrate to other places, that is, out-migration. Thus, four factors determine the growth of a population of a given society. These are: birth, death, immigration, and emigration. The actual growth of a given society between two points of time is represented by the following formula:

Population Growth = (Birth – Death) + (Immigration – Emigration)

According to the size and complexity of its composition, a society is classified into small or large, and homogeneous or heterogeneous. Indian society is a large and heterogeneous society. In terms of population, it is second only to China, though India's geographical landscape is only 2.4 per cent of the world surface area. The latest Census, which was completed at 0:00 hours on 1 March 2001, put the population of India at 1,027,015,247 or 1 billion and 27 million people.[2] China's population, at its last count (on 1 February 2000) was 1.277 billion). The United States of America (USA), which stands third in terms of population size, has only 281.4 million people (April 2000 count), which is 746 million short of the Indian population. Our two neighbours – Pakistan and Bangladesh – have 156.5 million and 129.2 million people, respectively. Since the global population stood at 6,055 million in 2000, the Indian population accounts for one-sixth (or 16.6%) of the world total.

It is important to know that systematic counting of the population in India started during the British regime. The period of modern, comprehensive censuses began in 1881. There is no dependable data about the earlier periods. However, efforts have been made by some demographers to estimate the size of population in earlier periods. These were based on accounts given by foreigners visiting the country, and on the literary works of those times. Some have also tried to guess the population by accounts of the size of the army of different kingdoms, taking a clue from the European countries, where the ratio of army personnel was 1:60, but this measure has been found to be defective. In any case, we must note that all figures of the pre-Census period are indirectly derived and are, therefore, only approximations. One estimate suggests that the population of India around 300 BC was between 100 and 140 million.[3] The estimates made by other scholars have put the population at around 125 million in 1600 AD (Kingsley Davis)[4] and 207 million in 1800 AD (Mahalanobis and Bhattacharya)[5]. It is interesting that both Kingsley Davis and Mahalanobis have made almost identical estimates about India's population in 1871 (255 and 256 million respectively). Mahalanobis and Bhattacharya suggest that between 1801 and 1871, the Indian population grew at the rate of 0.34 per cent per year. This increase is attributed to the peaceful conditions created during the British rule, when internecine wars, infighting, and banditry were greatly reduced. The slowdown in population growth between 1811-21 and 1831-41 was due to the higher mortality rates caused by the famines and epidemics that occurred during those decades.

The population of India at the time of the first Census, taken in the year 1881, was 253 million. In 1901, the population rose to 294 million. The 1941 Census, taken before the partition of India in 1947, put the population figure at 389 million. Taking out the areas that went to the newly created state of Pakistan, the revised total of what was left of India was 318 million in 1941. Partition meant a loss of nearly 70 million people; this is in terms of the 1941 Census figures for those areas that went to Pakistan. But it should be remembered that there was a huge influx of refugees from Pakistan who took shelter in India and, similarly, there was an exodus of Muslims from other parts of India to Pakistan. Thus, the actual size of India in 1947 will have to take note of both processes of migration – immigration and emigration.

From 318 million in 1941, independent India's population has reached the astounding figure of 1,027 million in 2001, registering an increase of 709 million people in a span of 60 years. This is more than three times the 1941 figure.

Conforming to the present territorial area of India, the Census data of the period, 1901-41, have been adjusted by the demographers to give a clear idea of the growth of the Indian population in various decades. In the following table, we present a comparative picture of the population of India in Census years 1901 to 2001.

Table 1

Population of India 1901-2001

Census Year	*Enumerated Population (Millions)*	*Intercensal Increase (Millions)*	*Percentage Increase*	*Average Annual Growth Rate (Percentage)*	*Density (Persons per Sq Km)*	*Sex Ratio (Females per 1,000 Males)*	*Urban Population (Percentage)*
1901	238.3				77	972	10.8
1911	252.0	13.6	5.75	0.56	82	964	10.3
1921	251.3	0.77	−0.31	−0.03	81	955	11.2
1931	278.9	27.6	11.00	1.05	90	950	12.0
1941	318.6	39.6	14.22	1.34	103	945	13.9
1951	361.0	42.4	13.31	1.26	117	946	17.3
1961	439.2	77.6	21.51	1.98	141	941	18.0
1971	548.1	108.9	24.80	2.24	178	930	19.9
1981	683.3	135.1	24.66	2.22	221	934	23.3
1991	843.3	163.0	23.86	2.14	267	927	25.7
2001	1027.0	180.6	21.34	1.93	324	933	27.8

Commenting on the growth pattern of the Indian population, the Census of India 2001 suggests that India's population growth during the 20th century can be classified into four distinct phases, as shown below:

1901-1921: Stagnant population
1921-1951: Steady growth
1951-1981: Rapid high growth
1981-2001: High growth with definite signs of slowing down

Figure 1
India: Decadal Growth of Population 1901-2001

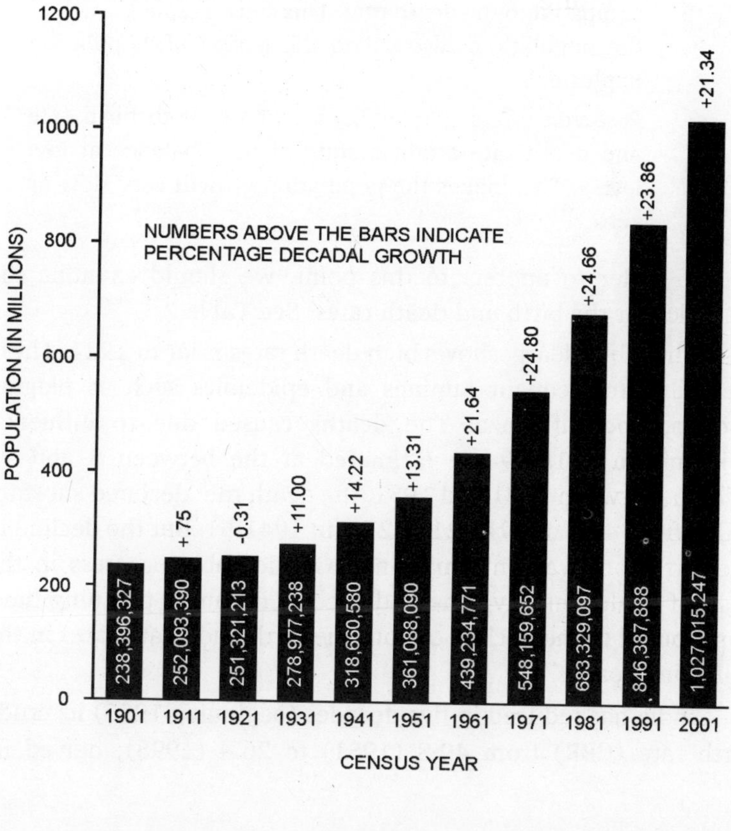

The Census of India 2001 shows that the 'story of population growth in India is fairly in tune with the classical theory of demographic transition'. According to this theory, the population of any given country passes through three distinct phases as shown below:

1. *Pre-transitional Phase:* In this phase, a society has high, almost matching, rates of births and deaths. This makes the population stationary, since the number of dead is replaced by the number of new-born. The rates indicate the number of persons per 1000 of the population.
2. *Transitional Phase:* In this phase, death rate begins to decline, while birth rate continues to be high, compared to the death rate. This causes rapid growth of the population. Also called the period of 'Population Explosion'.
3. *Post-transitional Phase:* In this phase, both birth rate and death rate attain a state of near balance at low levels. This makes the population growth very slow or zero.

In order to appreciate this point, we should examine the statistics for the birth and death rates. See Table 2.

The table clearly shows high death rates prior to 1921. These were due to frequent famines and epidemics such as plague, cholera, and influenza. The deaths caused due to influenza epidemic in 1918-19 are estimated at the between 8 and 15 million. Between 1921 and 1951, the death rate declined substantially, from 47.2 in 1911-21 to 27.4 in 1941-51. But the decline in the birth rate was only marginal. Considerable progress in the field of health and hygiene and success in family planning have contributed to the decline of both the birth and death rates in the following years.

India has reduced in five decades (beginning 1950) its crude birth rate (CBR) from 40.8 (1951) to 26.4 (1998); halved its

Table 2
Birth and Death Rates per 1,000 Population 1881-1998

Year	*Birth Rate*	*Death Rate*	*Natural Growth Rate*
1881-1891	48.9	41.3	7.6
1891-1901	45.8	44.4	1.4
1901-1911	49.2	42.6	6.6
1911-1921	48.1	47.2	0.9
1921-1931	46.4	36.3	10.1
1931-1941	45.2	31.2	14.0
1941-1951	39.9	27.4	12.5
1951-1961	41.7	22.8	18.9
1961-1971	41.1	18.9	22.2
1980-1982	33.8	12.1	21.5
1989-1990	30.8	10.3	20.5
1996-1998	27.0	9.0	18.0

infant mortality rate (IMR) from 146 per 1,000 live births (1951) to 72 per 1,000 live births (1998); quadrupled its couple protection rate (CPR) from 10.4 per cent (1971) to 44 per cent (1999); reduced its crude death rate (CDR) from 25 (1951) to 9.0 (1998); added 25 years to its life expectancy from 37 years to 62 years; achieved nearly universal awareness of the need for and methods of family planning, and reduced its total fertility rate from 6.0 (1951) to 3.3 (1997).

Population Density

India is regarded as an overpopulated country. The index for this is the relationship between land surface and the number of people. This gives us an idea of population density, defined as the

A crowded street

number of persons per square kilometre. According to the Census of 2001, the population density of India is 324 per sq. km. But this is the national average. The density varies from state to state, and ranges from 13 per sq. km. in Arunachal Pradesh to 9,294 per sq. km. in Delhi. The density of the Union territories is as follows: Chandigarh (7,903), Pondicherry (2,029), Lakshadweep (1,894), Daman and Diu (1,411), and Dadra and Nagar Haveli (449).

West Bengal tops the list of thickly populated states. Its population density is 904, followed by Bihar (880), Kerala (819), and Uttar Pradesh (689). The rest of the states can be grouped thus:

Between 400-500:	Punjab (482), Tamil Nadu (478), Haryana (477)
Between 300-400:	Goa (363), Assam (340), Jharkhand (338), Maharashtra (314), Tripura (304)

Between 200-300:	Andhra Pradesh (275), Karnataka (275), Gujarat (258), Orissa (236)
Between 100-200:	Madhya Pradesh (196), Rajasthan (165), Uttaranchal (159), Chhattisgarh (154), Nagaland (120), Himachal Pradesh (109), Manipur (107), Meghalaya (103)
Between 10-100:	Jammu & Kashmir (99), Sikkim (76), Andaman & Nicobar Islands (43), Mizoram (42), Arunachal Pradesh (13).

Population of Different States

The states within the Indian Union differ in terms of their population size. Uttar Pradesh (UP) remains the country's largest state, even after the creation of a separate hill state of Uttaranchal, which was formerly its part. According to the Census of 2001, UP's population is a huge 166 million people, constituting 16.17 per cent of India's population. The other nine most populated states are: Maharashtra (96.7 million), Bihar (82.8 million), West Bengal (80.2 million), Andhra Pradesh (75.72 million), Tamil Nadu (62.1 million), Madhya Pradesh (60.38 million), Rajasthan (56.47 million), Karnataka (52.73 million), and Gujarat (50.59 million). Lakshadweep is the smallest Union territory, with a population of only 60,595 people. Delhi's population (13.78 million) is larger than that of Jammu & Kashmir (10 million), Uttaranchal (8.4 million), and Himachal Pradesh (6.07 million). While Delhi represents 1.34 per cent of the country's population, these states are each represented by less than 1 per cent. The relative share of each of the states is shown in Figure 2.

Figure 2

Population Share of States and Union Territories in India: 2001

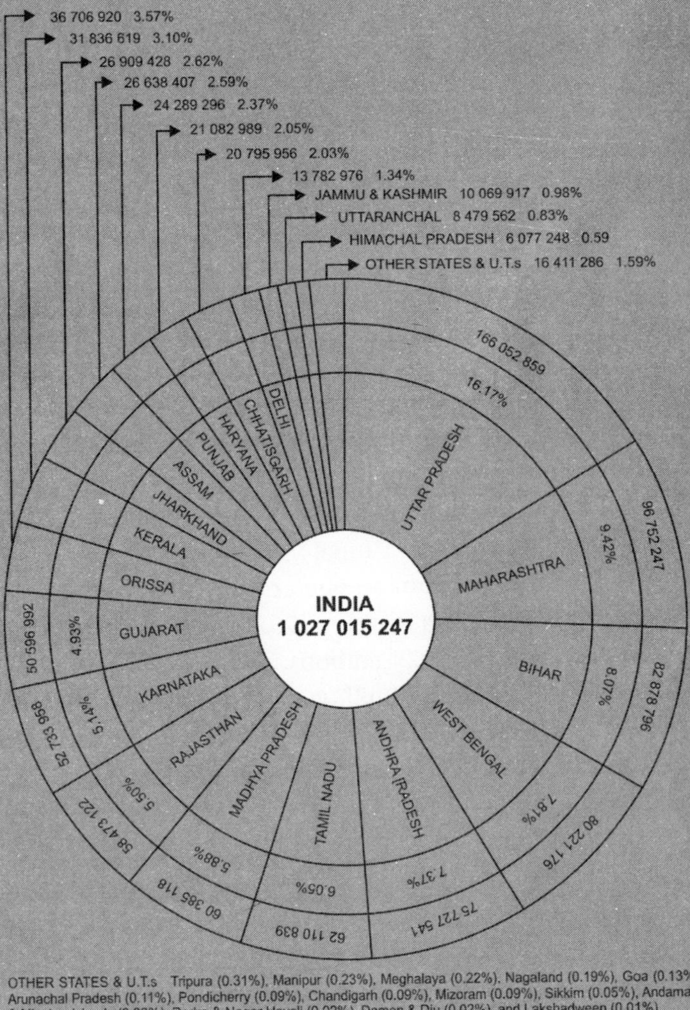

OTHER STATES & U.T.s Tripura (0.31%), Manipur (0.23%), Meghalaya (0.22%), Nagaland (0.19%), Goa (0.13%, Arunachal Pradesh (0.11%), Pondicherry (0.09%), Chandigarh (0.09%), Mizoram (0.09%), Sikkim (0.05%), Andaman & Micobar Islands (0.03%), Dadra & Nagar Haveli (0.02%), Damen & Diu (0.02%), and Lakshadweep (0.01%).

Sex Ratio

For the sociological analysis of a society, it is essential to know its sex composition, as this affects the incidence of marriage, birth, and death. A society gets its new members through sexual reproduction. Thus, it is important to have a balance between the two genders. This balance gets disturbed during wars, famines, or other calamities. It can also be affected by deliberate policy initiatives such as family planning. Migration also disturbs the sex ratio. For example, the migration of rural males to urban areas affects the sex ratio of both the rural and urban populations, and has implications for the families of the migrants, and settlement patterns of the places of migration.

World statistics show that per 1,000 males, there are 986 females; however, USA (1,029), Indonesia (1,004), Brazil (1,025), Russian Federation (1,140), Japan (1,041) and Nigeria (1,016) have more females than the male population. In case of India, as Table 1 has shown, the sex ratio is continuously declining, from 972 in 1901 to 933 in 2001. In 1991, it had reached an all time low of 927, but has picked up somewhat in the following decade. But it is still very low and is a cause for worry.

Analysing the trends in the last century, the Census Report for 2001 says:

> In 1901, there were as many as eleven states and Union territories that had a sex ratio of more than unity. Among these, except Kerala, all other states and Union territories have shown a downward slide. The major states that are largely responsible for the decline in the overall sex ratio in India are Uttar Pradesh, Bihar, Jharkhand, Orissa, Chhatisgarh, Madhya Pradesh, Gujarat, Maharashtra, and Tamil Nadu. Although the sex ratio in Punjab has been consistently low, it has shown a long-term upward trend and has not contributed to the overall deterioration in the sex ratio of the country. In Rajasthan, the sex ratio kept

fluctuating in a narrow band and always remained more or less stagnant. In West Bengal, the sex ratio declined sharply from 1901 to 1941 and then made a gradual turnaround on an upward path to reach 934 in 2001 [*Census of India 2001* Series 1, Provisional Population Totals: Paper 1 of 2001, page 91].

What the analysis suggests is the diversity in sex ratio among the states and Union territories. In 2001, the sex ratio ranged from 861 in Haryana to 1,058 in Kerala. Lower than the Haryana figures are those related to the Union territories: Chandigarh (773), Delhi (821), Daman & Diu (709), Dadra and Nagar Haveli (811), and Andaman & Nicobar Islands (818). Overall, there are eight states or Union territories (5.97% of India's total population) that have a sex ratio of below 880; four states (17.4% population), between 881 and 915; 11 states (47.23% population), between 916 and 950; eight states (18.08% population), between 951 and 985, and four states (11.27% population) have a high sex ratio of 985 and above. In other words, there are 17 states that have an above the national average sex ratio and 18 states that are below the national average of 933. The net deficit of women is over 35 million. Several highly populated states like Uttar Pradesh, Bihar, Rajasthan, and Madhya Pradesh, representing 36 per cent of India's population, are below the national average in this regard. A further breakdown of this data at the district level suggests wide variations in the sex ratio. The country is divided into 593 districts. Of these, 324 districts (55%) record a sex ratio of above 933. But 265 districts are below the national average and, among them, there are 23 districts where the ratio is as low as 833 or less. Only four districts correspond to the national average.

Religion-wise, sex ratio computations suggest that while the Hindu sex ratio (925) is closer to the national average of 933, it is dismally low in the case of Jains (870) and Sikhs (786). Birth rates of girls higher than the national average are recorded among Christians (964), Muslims (950), and Buddhists (942).

A survey conducted by the National Sample Survey Organization (NSS) in 2003-04, covering over one lakh families all over India suggests that while the sex ratio has improved in some Northern states (Haryana, Punjab, and Uttar Pradesh) it has witnessed a downward trend in Delhi and many Northeastern states. Delhi has gone down from 821 in 2001 to 808; Meghalaya, from 972 to 950; Manipur, from 978 to 932, and Mizoram, from 935 to 926. Himachal Pradesh (1,089) and Uttaranchal (1,014) have registered an improvement, while Kerala and Tamil Nadu have maintained a healthy sex ratio. The decline in sex ratio in the Union Territory of Delhi is mainly attributed to the failure of the health authorities to check female feticide.

Continuous decline in the sex ratio is a cause for worry. Social scientists have been alerted to the problem and are investigating the reasons. Demographic literature suggests many causes for the sex disparity in the population. These are sex ratios at birth (more male babies born per 1,000 female babies), sex differentials in mortality (more female babies dying in infancy), sex-differential migration (more male migrants), and under-enumeration of females. In the Indian context, it is alleged that because of a preference for the male child, many families indulged in female infanticide in the past – a practice that is deplored and is now nearly extinct. But there are complaints about the rise of female foeticide. Parents use sonography to determine the sex of the child in the womb and take recourse to abortion when the foetus is female. Measures are now being taken to stop this practice, which goes against human rights. However, it would be wrong to attribute the decline in sex ratio solely to female foeticide. But the worry about the decline in sex ratio is genuine and needs action on several fronts. It should be emphasized that the imbalance in the sex ratio poses a threat to the very survival of society. After all, it is through sexual reproduction that a society continually renews its membership. The institutions of marriage, family, and kinship are all dependent upon the sexual composition of the society.

The Children and the Aged

The Children

According to the theory of demographic transition, during the second phase of transition, the population in the younger and older age groups begins to show signs of increase, technically called 'bulges'. Because of the decline in the death rate and relatively slow decline in the birth rate, fewer children die at birth or in infancy; similarly, the average age jumps because of the increasing longevity. This results in an increase in the number of people who are aged 60 and above. But with greater decline in fertility, the bulge at the lower end starts getting smaller, while the one at the upper end goes on inflating. This can be seen from Indian data.

Children in the age group of 0-6 years constituted 17.94 per cent of the population in 1991. This percentage has come down in 2001 to 15.42. There are now 157.8 million children, of which 81.91 million are boys and 75.95 million girls. This gives us the sex ratio of 927. The decline in the number of female children is indeed a cause for worry. From 976 in 1961, the sex ratio among children in the age group of 0-6 years has come down to 964 in 1971, and 962 in 1981. It came further down to 945 in 1991 and to 927 in 2001. What is worse is the fact that in the affluent areas of Punjab (790), Haryana (820), Chandigarh (845), Himachal Pradesh (897), Gujarat (878) and Delhi (865) the ratio is even lower.

The data regarding sex ratio of children in the age group of 0-6 years in 591 districts of the country show that in as many as

121 districts, this ratio is below 900 (in fact, in 16 districts, it is below 800).[6] There are only 12 districts where the number of girl children is higher than that of the male children.[7] Table 3 shows the distribution of districts by sex ratio among young children.

Table 3

Sex Ratio in the Age Group of 0-6 Years in Various Districts of India

Sex Ratio	*Number of Districts*
Less than 800	16
800-849	33
850-899	72
900-949	213
950-999	245
1,000-1,049	12
Total	591

Social workers and politicians attribute the decline in the sex ratio among children to the tendency towards female foeticide, which is helped by the unethical practice of using techniques such as ultrasound and amniocentesis to determine the sex of a foetus. The government enacted the Pre-conception and Pre-natal Diagnostic Techniques (Prohibition of Sex Selection) Act in 1994, but it has not been effectively implemented. With the advent of more sophisticated techniques like sperm separation, it is becoming harder to curb female foetus elimination practices.

The Older People

In India, the number and the percentage of older people are rising. The growing bulge at the upper end of the age pyramid is

Figure 3
Population Pyramids of India

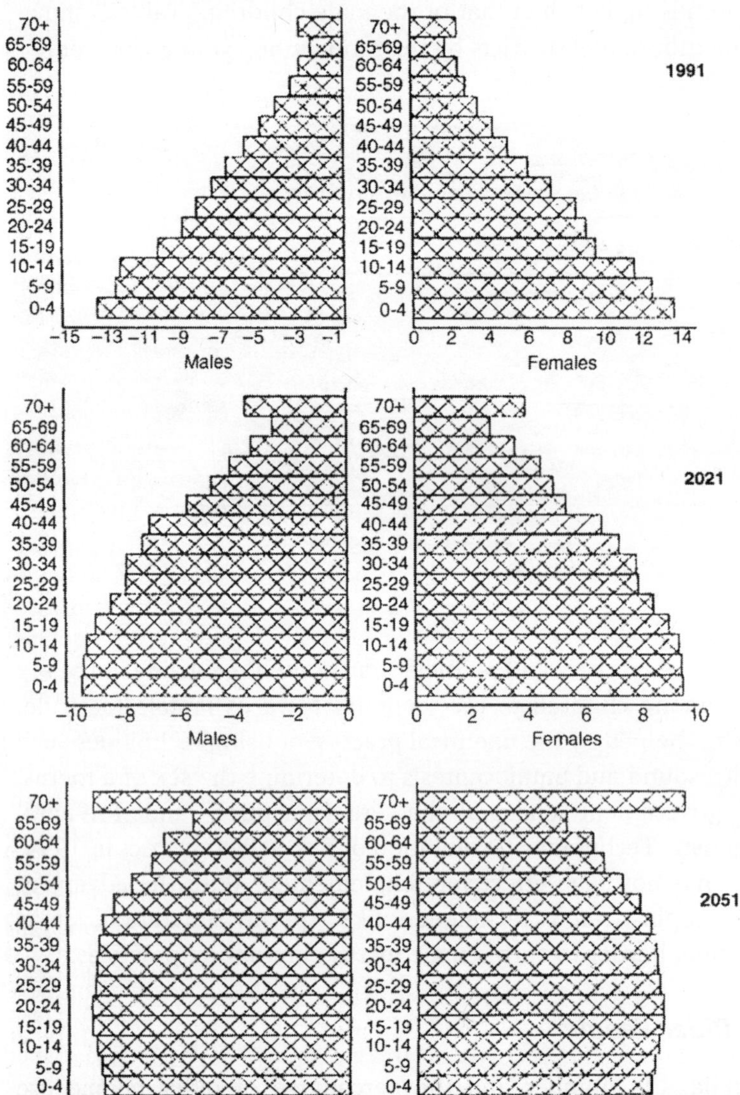

An ageing Indian

Village woman showing her old-age pension papers

clearly visible. It may be recalled that life expectancy was around 25 years in 1901; it is now nearly 65. This is why, in 1901, a person above the age of 60 was expected to live for another 9 years. In 1951, this expectation increased to 10.9 years for men and 11.4 years for women and, in 1991, these figures changed to 17.3 for men and 18 for women. The size of the older population is likely to further rise in the coming years. It was 56.7 million (6.8% of the population) in 1991. The number of older persons in 2001 was estimated at 76 million. This figure is likely to reach 177 million by 2021. The United Nations (UN) has projected that India's population in the 60+ age group is likely to be 198 million in 2030, and climb to 326 million by 2050, when it will constitute 21 per cent of the total population. It is interesting to note that while it took France 115 years to double the number of its elderly from 7 to 14 per cent, in Japan, this occurred in just 26 years, between 1970 and 1996. In other developing countries, including India, this doubling period is going to be much shorter. Already, our elderly population is around 12.6 per cent.

The point to be noted is that the population of both children and older people is rising. In 1991, there were 18.4 elderly persons for every 100 children; in 2001, this ratio changed to 24.7 elderly persons per 100 children. This means that the society has to pay attention, not only to the needs of the increasing child population, but also to the continually increasing older population.

Because of the worldwide concern for the growing elderly population, the UN observed 1999 as the International Year of the Older Persons. Every year, first day of October is celebrated as the Day of the Older Persons. The UN slogan for the Day is: "To add life to the years that have been added to life."

The government of India adopted the National Policy for Older Persons in 1999. The policy took a comprehensive view of the needs of the aged. It enjoins the state and civil society to extend support for financial security, healthcare, shelter, and other needs of older persons, provide protection against abuse and exploitation, and to empower them. A Five-Year Plan of Action from 2000 to 2005 was drawn up to identify the role of the state governments and the Central government in implementing the National Policy for Older Persons and to review its implementation every three years.

Some key emphases in the Policy are:

- Facilitating partnership amongst government, civil society, and the private sector;
- Ensuring financial security in old age;
- Recognizing the aged as a resource pool;
- Better healthcare facilities for all older persons;
- Extending proper protection, security and legal rights; and
- Commitment to gender equality in the programmes for the aged.

Recognizing the importance of financial security, the Government of India commissioned a national project called 'Old Age Social and Income Security' (OASIS) in 1999 with a view to drawing up a comprehensive plan for the financial security of workers on retirement and old age in sectors where no formal arrangements exist.

Population Distribution

Another question of vital interest is: Where do the people in a country reside? As we know, prior to independence, the country was divided into British India and the princely states, which owed their allegiance to the Crown. British India consisted of 11 provinces and six other territories. The princely states numbered 560. Partition of India at the time of independence changed the political geography of the country, as some parts went to the newly created state of Pakistan. But gradually, the princely states merged with the Indian Union, requiring a fresh division of them into states. The new states and Union territories numbered 29 and were classified into A, B, C states and D territories. In 1956, the states were reorganized, abolishing the various distinctions and grouped only as states and Union territories. These are now grouped into the Northern, Eastern, Central, Western, and Southern zones. Recently, on popular demand, some bigger states were bifurcated with the creation of Uttaranchal (formerly part of Uttar Pradesh), Chhatisgarh (formerly part of Madhya Pradesh), and Jharkhand (formerly part of Bihar). Today, the country is divided into 28 states and seven Union territories. These states and territories differ in their land area and population size. Administratively, each state is further divided into districts. There are 593 districts. Thus, the population of India is divided into various districts within 28 states and seven Union territories.

From village to town

Each district is further divided into various settlements that are either rural or urban. We shall discuss the special features of the rural and urban settlements in a later chapter, but here we shall analyse the distribution of the population in terms of their rural or urban residence. It must be said here that the definition of what constitutes an urban settlement has not been the same in all the censuses, which makes comparison somewhat difficult.

Table 4 gives the distribution of the population into rural and urban for the period, 1901-2001.

Table 4

Rural and Urban Population 1901-2001

Census Year	*Rural (Millions)*	*Percentage of the Total*	*Urban (Millions)*	*Percentage of the Total*	*Total Population*
1901	213	89.2	26	10.8	239
1911	226	89.7	26	10.3	252
1921	223	88.8	28	11.2	251
1931	246	88.0	33	12.0	279
1941	275	86.1	44	13.9	319
1951	299	82.7	62	17.3	361
1961	360	82.0	79	18.0	439
1971	439	80.1	109	19.9	548
1981	524	76.7	159	23.3	683
1991	629	74.3	218	25.7	847
2001	742	72.2	285	27.8	1,027

These figures indicate that India continues to be predominantly rural, with 72.2 per cent of its population residing in rural areas. Rural settlements number 5,80,781 ranging from those that have a population of over 10,000 persons to those with less than even 500 people. While the urban population still constitutes only

27 per cent of the total, it accounts for 285 million people, which incidentally was the population of the entire country in the decade of 1941-50, and which is much larger than the total population of Pakistan or Indonesia today.

There is clear evidence of a growing urban population. But this growth is uneven. There is high incidence of urban population in the Union territories of Chandigarh (89.78%), Delhi (93.01%), and Pondicherry (66.57%). Barring Dadra and Nagar Haveli (which has only 22.89% urban population), the other Union territories also have an urban population the percentage of which is higher than the national average, but considerably lower than Chandigarh, Delhi, and Pondicherry; thus, Daman and Diu has a 36.26 per cent urban population, Lakshadweep has 44.47 per cent, and Andaman and Nicobar Islands have 32.67 per cent.

Only five of the states come in the upper bracket with their urban population share ranging between 37 and 49 per cent; these are: Goa (49.77%), Mizoram (49.50%), Tamil Nadu (43.86%), Maharashtra (42.40%), and Gujarat (37.35%).

Another five states fall in the middle range, with an urban population of between 27 and 36 per cent. These are Punjab and Karnataka (each with 33.9% urban population), Haryana (29%), West Bengal (28.03%), and Andhra Pradesh (27.08%).

States having an urban population of between 17 and 26 per cent are Kerala (25.97%), Uttaranchal (25.59%), Jammu & Kashmir (24.8%), Manipur (23.86%), Rajasthan (23.38%), Jharkhand (22.5%), Uttar Pradesh (20.78%), Arunachal (20.41%), Chhattisgarh (20.08%), Meghalaya (19.63%), Nagaland (17.74%), and Tripura (17.02%). It is interesting to note that some of the areas with a high concentration of tribals, particularly in the Northeast, show high incidence of urbanization.

The following states continue to be largely rural with 15 per cent or less urban population: Orissa (14.97%), Assam (12.22%),

Sikkim (11.10%), Bihar (10.47%), and Himachal Pradesh (9.79%).

India has 23 mega cities that have a population of more than one million. According to the 1991 Census, the biggest city was Greater Mumbai, with a population of 12.59 million, followed by Kolkata (11.02 million), Delhi (8.42 million), and Chennai (5.42 million). At the lower end are the cities of Madurai, Bhopal, Visakhapatanam, Ludhiana, and Varanasi (each with a little more than one million population).

Population by Religion

The country is inhabited by people belonging to different religions and sects. This is a good indicator of India's multi-culturalism. People are broadly grouped into Hindus, Muslims, Christians, Sikhs, Buddhists, Jains and Others (those who are very small in number and unclassified). Though Census 2001 totals by religion are still not available, the 1991 data are good enough to assess their relative preponderance. The new figures are only likely to affect the actual numbers and not the percentage distribution by religion. Table 5 gives the distribution of population by religion in the years 1961 and 1991, which clearly shows that the relative proportion of the various religious groups has remained more or less the same.

As the data indicate, the country is preponderantly Hindu. But the Hindus do not constitute a single group. There are various sects in it; people belonging to these sects also maintain their distinct identity. However, people ignore the sectarian differences in their day-to-day dealings and thus club not only Hindus belonging to different sects, but also Sikhs and Jains, and even Buddhists, into a common category. All political differences between communities are polarized between the Hindus and the Muslims. Researchers working in villages and towns have also

Table 5

Population by Religion 1961-1991

Religious Group	*1961*		*1991*	
	Number	*Percentage*	*Number*	*Percentage*
Hindus	366.5	83.5	672.6	82.41
Muslims	46.9	10.7	95.2	11.67
Christians	10.7	2.4	18.9	2.32
Sikhs	7.8	1.8	16.3	1.99
Buddhists	3.2	0.7	6.3	0.77
Jains	2.0	0.5	3.4	0.41
Others	1.6	0.4	3.5	0.43

discovered many Hindus worshipping Muslim *Pirs* and visiting the *Mazars* (tombs) of Muslim saints. Many Hindu names have Arabic words, such as Iqbal Narain, Daulat Ram, Bakshi Lal, Mulayam Singh, Fateh Singh, and Roshan Lal. Similarly, mixed names are also found among Muslims such as Ashroff Adiraja. Many of our top film stars have adopted Hindu names, and are better known by them such as Dilip Kumar, Sanjay Khan, Madhubala, and Meena Kumari. Caste groups that have converted from Hinduism to other religions did not give up their caste names. Thus, Jats and Tyagis are found both among the Hindus and Muslims. These serve as good examples of intermingling while maintaining separate identities. However, politicization of religion has generated tendencies of communalism in the country, which work to destroy the spirit of harmony and co-living among the people practising different religions. In political jargon, the Hindus are regarded as a majority community, constituting 82.41 per cent of the population, and all others are called minorities. In the context of India, even the minorities have a substantial population. For example, the Muslims may be called a minority because they are only 11.67 per cent of the population, but this percentage represents more than 95 million people. The Sikh population, which constitutes only 1.99 per cent, is as large as the population of all of Australia. The Jains in India are larger in number than the population of New Zealand. Such huge numbers of different religious groups significantly affect inter-communal relations.

There is another point: While there are some pockets of concentration of the various minority groups in terms of states, districts, and even wards in the cities, each of these units is pluri-religious in demographic composition. Thus, the social structure of the various territorial units represents this diversity and demonstrates the manner in which the system of relationships operates. It is in this sense that the Indian social system is not synonymous with the Hindu social system.

Literacy Profile

Literacy is broadly defined as the ability to read and write. Since children in the age group of 0-6 years are not expected to acquire these skills, the Census treats them as 'illiterate'. Thus, the literacy data relate to the population aged seven years and above only. "For the purposes of census, a person aged seven and above, who can both read and write with understanding in any language, is treated as literate. A person who can only read, but cannot write, is not literate" (Census of India 2001, Series 1, Paper 1 of 2001, page 105). However, it "is not mandatory that to be treated as literate, a person should have received any formal education or acquired any minimum educational standard. Literacy status can be acquired through adult literacy classes or by attending any non-formal educational system. Persons who are unfortunately blind and read in Braille are also treated as literates" (ibid.). Since 1991, the literacy rate is computed only for the population

Open-air class in a village

relating to seven years and above. In earlier censuses this rate was computed by taking into account the total population. This change in the procedure also partially accounts for a better literacy rate in the later years.

Table 6
Literacy Rate in India 1951-2001

Census Year	*Persons*	*Males*	*Females*	*Male-Female Gap in Literacy Rate*
1	*2*	*3*	*4*	*5*
1951	18.33	27.16	8.86	18.30
1961	28.30	40.40	15.35	25.05
1971	34.45	45.96	21.97	23.98
1981	43.57	56.38	29.76	26.62
1991	52.21	64.13	39.29	24.84
2001	65.38	75.85	54.18	21.70

The literacy profile of India has greatly changed since independence. In 1947, the country's literates constituted a bare 16 per cent of the total population. The 1991 Census reported a 52.2 per cent literacy rate. A further advance has been made in the last decade and the literacy rate, according to the 2001 Census, stands at 65.38 per cent. Literates number 566,714,995 of which 339,969,048 are males and 226,745,947 females. More than 203 million people have been added to the 1991 figure in the category of literates; of these, 108 million are males and 96 million females. This suggests that the gender gap is closing steadily.

The comparison of the 1991 and 2001 figures tell yet another story. Earlier in India, as is the case in many developing countries, while the percentage of illiterates continued to decline, the actual numbers showed a rising trend. From this angle, the 2001 figures come as a great relief. Not only has the percentage of illiterates declined but their number is significantly smaller than the 1991 figures. The total number of illiterates in 1991 was 328 million; that number now stands at 296 million, a decline of 32 million. This fact signifies not only the success of the efforts to eradicate illiteracy, it also implies that we will have a continually declining size of target population for purposes of achieving universal literacy. In developing any programme of education, however, one will have to think, not only of illiterates in the population above the age of seven years, but also about the youngest age group that will have to be provided schooling. The 2001 Census indicates that the age group 0-6 years represents 15.42 per cent of the population, with an absolute number of 157 million. Thus, the educational enterprise has to respond to the need for literacy for a combined total of 453 million (157 children in the age group of 0-6 years and 296 million illiterates in the 7+ category). The challenge of eradicating illiteracy from India is indeed huge. India is one of the nine giants in the world in terms of a mammoth population of illiterates with high incidence of illiteracy among females.

The Census results of 2001 show that the number of literates has more than doubled in the Union territory of Dadra and Nagar Haveli and in the state of Rajasthan during the last decade. Other states that have shown decadal percentage increase of more than 80 are Nagaland (85.6%), Chhattisgarh (85.25%), Madhya Pradesh (83.69%), Daman and Diu (83.22%), and Uttar Pradesh (81.75%).

Seeing it from the point of view of illiteracy, it is a matter of great relief that the absolute number of illiterates in the country as a whole has declined by 31,958,336 in the decade, 1991-2001. The maximum decline in number of illiterates occurred in Andhra Pradesh, followed by Uttar Pradesh, Maharashtra, Rajasthan, Madhya Pradesh, and Tamil Nadu. These together account for a 75 per cent decrease. On the other hand, the number of illiterates have increased in Bihar, Delhi, Nagaland, Manipur, and Chandigarh.

Decrease in illiteracy is seen among both males and females. Among males, the decrease in absolute numbers is 21,445,145, and among females, 10,513,191. The highest decrease in male illiteracy was registered in Uttar Pradesh (19.46% of the total decrease), followed by Andhra Pradesh (13.59%), Rajasthan (12.42%), and Madhya Pradesh (11.37%). The maximum number of illiterates has increased in Bihar from 13,128,759 in 1991 to 13,799,477 in 2001 (an increase of 670,718). Surprisingly, the state of Kerala, which tops in male literacy, has also shown a marginal increase of 2,412 among male illiterates. Among the females, the maximum decrease is registered in the state of Andhra Pradesh (a decrease of 2,451,160 compared to the 1991 figure). Other states showing significant decrease in the number of female illiterates are Maharashtra, Tamil Nadu, Madhya Pradesh, and West Bengal. All these states taken together account for 82.69 per cent of the total decline in female illiteracy figures as compared to 1991.

From the above, it should be clear that there are wide-ranging differences in terms of the literacy profile between the different states and Union territories. The Census of India 2001 concludes: "Kerala continues to occupy the top spot in the country, both in male literacy with 94.20 per cent and female literacy with 87.86 per cent. On the other hand, Bihar has recorded the lowest literacy rates both in case of males (60.32%) and females (33.57%). Seven states/Union territories having less than 50 per cent female literacy rates are Rajasthan (44.34%), Arunachal Pradesh (44.24%), Dadra and Nagar Haveli (42.99%), Uttar Pradesh (42.98%), Jammu and Kashmir (41.82%), Jharkhand (39.38%), and Bihar (33.57%)."

Overall, Andhra Pradesh, Arunachal Pradesh, Assam, Bihar, Chhatisgarh, Dadra and Nagar Haveli, Jammu and Kashmir, Jharkhand, Madhya Pradesh Meghalaya, Orissa, Rajasthan, and Uttar Pradesh have literacy rates that are below the national average.

Census 2001 reports that the highest visible improvement in male literacy rate is noticed in Rajasthan with a difference of 21.47 percentage points. In female literacy, too, Rajasthan has fared well (23.90 percentage points) although Chhatisgarh has the lead here with a difference of 24.87 percentage points. While there is no state or Union territory that has a male literacy rate of below 60 per cent in 2001 (there were 10 in the 50-60 per cent group in 1991), there are 15 states/Union territories that have a female literacy rate below this figure; of these, two are in the range of 0-40 per cent, four in the range of 40-50 per cent, and nine in the range of 50-60 per cent. The redeeming feature is that in 1991, there were 26 states/Union territories that had a below 60 per cent female literacy rate Thus, 11 states have moved up with better female literacy rates.

Such data are helpful in locating the areas and groups that suffer from illiteracy so that suitable programmes can be developed for these regions.

A Note on the National Population Policy

India being a highly populated country, the government has continuously paid attention to the problem of population growth. Just a few months before the attainment of independence in 1946, the Bhore Committee submitted its Report, which became the basis for developing a population policy. This was followed by the launch of the Family Planning Programme in 1952, coinciding with the launch of the nationwide Community Development Programme. After careful review of the demographic trends and of the Family Planning Programme, in 1976, the government issued its first statement regarding the National Population Policy, which was followed by the 1977 Policy Statement on the Family Welfare Programme. It was in 1983 that the government adopted the National Health Policy, which emphasized the need for 'securing the small family norm through voluntary efforts and moving towards the goal of population stabilization'. While adopting the Health Policy, the Parliament underscored the need for a separate National Population Policy. Accordingly, the National Development Council appointed a Committee on Population in 1991 under the chairmanship of Karunakaran, which submitted its report in 1993, recommending the formulation of a National Population Policy to take a 'a long-term holistic view of development, population growth, and environmental protection' and to 'suggest policies and guidelines [for] formulation of programmes' and 'a monitoring mechanism with short- medium- and long-term perspectives and goals'. Subsequently, an Expert Group headed by M.S. Swaminathan was appointed to prepare the draft of a national population policy. The National Population Policy (NPP) finally came into force in 2000.

The Policy states that the "immediate objective of the NPP 2000 is to address the unmet needs for contraception, healthcare infrastructure, and health personnel, and to provide integrated service delivery for basic reproductive and child healthcare. The medium-term objective is to bring the Total Fertility Rate (TFR) to replacement levels by the year 2010, through vigorous implementation of inter-sectoral operational strategies. The long-term objective of the Policy is to achieve a stable population by 2045, at a level consistent with the requirements of sustainable economic growth, social development, and environmental protection."

The NPP has listed the following goals for 2010:

1. Address the unmet needs for basic reproductive and child health services, supplies, and infrastructure;
2. Make school education up to age 14 free and compulsory, and reduce dropouts at the primary and secondary school levels to below 20 per cent for both boys and girls;
3. Reduce the infant mortality rate to below 30 per 1,000 live births;
4. Reduce the maternal mortality ratio to below 100 per 100,000 live births;
5. Achieve universal immunization of children against all vaccine preventable diseases;
6. Promote delayed marriage for girls, not earlier than age 18 and preferably after 20 years of age;
7. Achieve 80 per cent institutional deliveries and 100 per cent deliveries by trained persons;
8. Achieve universal access to information/counselling, and services for fertility regulation and contraception with a wide basket of choices;
9. Achieve 100 per cent registration of births, deaths, marriages, and pregnancy;
10. Contain the spread of the Acquired Immuno-deficiency Syndrome (AIDS) and promote greater integration between the management of reproductive tract infections (RTIs) and sexually transmitted infections (STIs) and the National AIDS Control Organization;
11. Prevent and control communicable diseases;

12. Integrate Indian Systems of Medicine (ISM) in the provision of reproductive and child health services, and in reaching out to households; and
13. Promote vigorously the small family norm to achieve replacement levels of TFR. Bring about convergence in implementation of related social-sector programmes so that family welfare becomes a people-centred programme.

The NPP 2000 anticipates that proper implementation of this policy will help limit the population to 1,107 million (110 crores) in 2010, instead of 1,162 million (116 crores) as projected by the Technical Group on Population Projections. It is hoped that the TFR will reach the replacement level of 2.1 by 2010. The long-term objective of achieving a stable population by 2045, at a level consistent with the requirements of sustainable economic growth, social development, and environment protection will also require considerable effort and efficient implementation of the NPP.

Concluding Remarks

Population plays an important role in a country's economic and social development, measured in terms of quality of life and the well-being of its people. Sharply increasing numbers of people put a strain on the country's resource base and increase its dependence on outside support. India already has 16 per cent of the world's population on 2.4 per cent of the globe's land area. It is projected that if current trends are not stemmed, India may overtake China by 2045 as the most populous country.[8] "While the global population has increased threefold during this century, from two billion to six billion, the population of India has increased nearly five times from 238 million (23 crores) to one billion in the same period. India's current annual increase in population of 15.5 million is large enough to neutralize efforts to conserve the resource endowment and environment."

For promoting sustainable development with more equitable distribution, it is necessary to stabilize the population. But this should be done in such a fashion that we do not disturb the gender balance. The changing demographic scenario also requires reconsideration of our priorities towards the children and the elderly, whose numbers and proportion are continually rising.

Appendix 1

India: Population Figures at a Glance
Census of India 2001
Provisional Population Totals

Population[9]	Persons	1,027,015,247	
	Males	531,277,078	
	Females	495,738,169	
Decadal Population		Absolute	Percentage
Growth 1991-2001	Persons	180,627,359	21.34
	Males	91,944,020	20.93
	Females	88,683,339	21.79
Density of Population[10] (per sq. km.)	324		
Sex Ratio (Females per 1,000 Males)	933		
Population in the Age Group Years 0-6		Absolute	Percentage to Total Population
	Persons	157,863,145	15.42
	Males	81,911,041	15.47
	Females	75,952,104	15.36
Literates		Absolute	Percentage to Total Population
	Persons	566,714,995	65.38
	Males	339,969,048	75.85
	Females	226,745,947	54.16

Appendix 2

Rural-Urban Distribution of Population–India and States/Union Territories 2001

S. No.	India/State/ Union Territory*	T/ R/ U	Population Persons	Males	Females	Percent Urban Population
1	2	3	5	6	7	8
	India	T	1,027,015,247	531,277,078	495,738,169	27.78
		R	741,660,293	381,141,184	360,519,109	
		U	285,354,954	150,135,894	135,219,060	
	State/Union Territory*					
1	Jammu & Kashmir	T	10,069,917	5,300,574	4,769,343	24.88
		R	7,564,608	3,925,846	3,638,762	
		U	2,505,309	1,374,728	1,130,581	
2	Himachal Pradesh	T	6,077,248	3,085,256	2,991,992	9.79
		R	5,482,367	2,754,251	2,728,116	
		U	594,881	331,005	263,876	
3	Punjab	T	24,289,296	12,963,362	11,325,934	33.95
		R	16,043,730	8,500,647	7,543,083	
		U	8,245,566	4,462,715	3,782,851	
4	Chandigarh*	T	900,914	508,224	392,690	89.78
		R	92,118	56,837	35,281	
		U	808,796	451,387	357,409	
5	Uttaranchal	T	8,479,562	4,316,401	4,163,161	25.59
		R	6,309,317	3,143,380	3,165,937	
		U	2,170,245	1,173,021	997,224	
6	Haryana	T	21,082,989	11,327,658	9,755,331	29.00
		R	14,968,850	8,017,622	6,951,228	
		U	6,114,139	3,310,036	2,804,103	
7	Delhi*	T	13,782,976	7,570,890	6,212,086	93.01
		R	963,215	533,219	429,996	
		U	12,819,761	7,037,671	5,782,090	
8	Rajasthan	T	56,473,122	29,381,657	27,091,465	23.38
		R	43,267,678	22,394,479	20,873,199	
		U	13,205,444	6,987,178	6,218,266	

Contd...

Contd...

9	Uttar Pradesh	T	166,052,859	87,466,301	78,586,558	20.78
		R	131,540,230	69,096,765	62,443,465	
		U	34,512,629	18,369,536	16,143,093	
10	Bihar	T	82,878,796	43,153,964	39,724,832	10.47
		R	74,199,596	38,510,686	35,688,910	
		U	8,679,200	4,643,278	4,035,922	
11	Sikkim	T	540,493	288,217	252,276	11.10
		R	480,488	255,386	225,102	
		U	60,005	32,831	27,174	
12	Arunachal Pradesh	T	1,091,117	573,951	517,166	20.41
		R	868,429	453,560	414,869	
		U	222,688	120,391	102,297	
13	Nagaland	T	1,988,636	1,041,686	946,950	17.74
		R	1,635,815	846,651	789,164	
		U	352,821	195,035	157,786	
14	Manipur	T	2,388,634	1,207,338	1,181,296	23.88
		R	1,818,224	923,428	894,796	
		U	570,410	283,910	286,500	
15	Mizoram	T	891,058	459,783	431,275	49.50
		R	450,018	233,718	216,300	
		U	441,040	226,065	214,975	
16	Tripura	T	3,191,168	1,636,138	1,555,030	17.02
		R	2,648,074	1,359,288	1,288,786	
		U	543,094	276,850	266,244	
17	Meghalaya	T	2,306,069	1,167,840	1,138,229	19.63
		R	1,853,457	939,803	913,654	
		U	452,612	228,037	224,575	
18	Assam	T	26,638,407	13,787,799	12,850,608	12.72
		R	23,248,994	11,983,157	11,265,837	
		U	3,389,413	1,804,642	1,584,771	
19	West Bengal	T	80,221,171	41,487,694	38,733,477	28.03
		R	57,734,690	29,606,028	28,128,662	
		U	22,486,481	11,881,666	10,604,815	

Contd...

Contd...

20	Jharkhand	T	26,909,428	13,861,277	13,048,151	22.25
		R	20,922,731	10,660,430	10,262,301	
		U	5,986,697	3,200,847	2,785,850	
21	Orissa	T	36,706,920	18,612,340	18,094,580	14.97
		R	31,210,602	15,711,853	15,498,749	
		U	5,496,318	2,900,487	2,595,831	
22	Chhatisgarh	T	20,795,956	10,452,426	10,343,530	20.08
		R	16,620,627	8,290,983	8,329,644	
		U	4,175,329	2,161,443	2,013,886	
23	Madhya Pradesh	T	60,385,118	31,456,873	28,928,245	26.67
		R	44,282,528	22,975,256	21,307,272	
		U	16,102,590	8,481,617	7,620,973	
24	Gujarat	T	50,596,992	26,344,053	24,252,939	37.35
		R	31,697,615	16,289,423	15,408,192	
		U	18,899,377	10,054,630	8,844,747	
25	Daman & Diu*	T	158,059	92,478	65,581	36.26
		R	100,740	63,576	37,164	
		U	57,319	28,902	28,417	
26	Dadra & Nagar Haveli*	T	220,451	121,731	98,720	22.89
		R	169,995	91,887	78,108	
		U	50,456	29,844	20,612	
27	Maharashtra	T	96,752,247	50,334,270	46,417,977	42.40
		R	55,732,513	28,443,238	27,289,275	
		U	41,019,734	21,891,032	19,128,702	
28	Andhra Pradesh	T	75,727,541	38,286,811	37,440,730	27.08
		R	55,223,944	27,852,179	27,371,765	
		U	20,503,597	10,434,632	10,068,965	
29	Karnataka	T	52,733,958	26,856,343	25,877,615	33.98
		R	34,814,100	17,618,593	17,195,507	
		U	17,919,858	9,237,750	8,682,108	
30	Goa	T	1,343,998	685,617	658,381	49.77
		R	675,129	339,626	335,503	
		U	668,869	345,991	322,878	

Contd...

Contd...

31	Lakshadweep*	T	60,595	31,118	29,477	44.47
		R	33,647	17,196	16,451	
		U	26,948	13,922	13,026	
32	Kerala	T	31,838,619	15,468,664	16,369,955	25.97
		R	23,571,484	11,450,785	12,120,699	
		U	8,267,135	4,017,879	4,249,256	
33	Tamil Nadu	T	62,110,839	31,268,654	30,842,185	43.86
		R	34,869,286	17,508,985	17,360,301	
		U	27,241,553	13,759,669	13,481,884	
34	Pondicherry*	T	973,829	486,705	487,124	66.57
		R	325,596	163,586	162,010	
		U	648,233	323,119	325,114	
35	Andaman & Nicobar Islands*	T	356,265	192,985	163,280	32.67
		R	239,858	128,837	111,021	
		U	116,407	64,148	52,259	

Notes: 1. The total, rural and urban population of India includes the estimated total, rural and urban population of entire Kachchh district, Morvi, Maliya-Miyana and Wankaner taluks of Rajkot district, Jodiya taluka of Jamnagar district of Gujarat state and estimated total and rural population of entire Kinnaur district of Himachal Pradesh where population enumeration of Census of India, 2001 could not be conducted due to natural calamities.

2. The figures of total, rural and urban population of Himachal Pradesh state have been arrived at after including the estimated total and rural population of entire Kinnaur district, where population enumeration of Census of India, 2001 could not be conducted due to natural calamity.

3. The figures of total, rural and urban population of Gujarat state have been arrived at after including the estimated total, rural and urban population of entire Kachchh district, Morvi, Maliya-Miyana and Wankaner taluks of Rajkot district, Jodiya taluka of Jamnagar district, where population enumeration of the Census of India, 2001 could not be conducted due to natural calamity.

Notes

1. The Greek word, *dcmos,* stands for people and 'graphy' is derived from the Latin *graphia* or Greek *graphein,* meaning to write or record. Together, the two words are used for a descriptive science, thus demography is the descriptive science of human populations.
2. One billion equals 1,000 million, or 100 crores, or 1 arab.
3. Pran Nath, *A Study in the Economic Conditions of Ancient India*, 1929, Royal Asiatic Society, London, p. 122.
4. Kingsley Davis, *The Population of India and Pakistan*, 1951, Princeton University Press, Chapter IV.
5. P.C. Mahalanobis and D. Bhattacharya, 'Growth of Population in India and Pakistan, 1801-1961', *Artha Vinjana*, March 1976.
6. 10 of these districts are in Punjab, five in Haryana, and one in Gujarat.
7. These districts fall in Arunachal Pradesh (2), Chhatisgarh (2, both tribal), Jammu & Kashmir (4), Sikkim, Manipur, Nagaland, and Orissa (one each).
8. India's population in 1991 and the projections up to 2016 are as follows:

   March 1991: 846.3 milllion

   March 2001: 1,012.4 million

   March 2011: 1,178.9 million

   March 2016: 1,263.5 million
9. The population of India includes the estimated population of the entire Kachchh district, Morvi, Maliya-Miyana and Wankaner taluks of Rajkot district, Jodiya taluk of Jamnagar district of Gujarat and the entire Kinnaur district of Himachal Pradesh, where the population enumeration of the Census of India 2001 could not be conducted due to natural calamities.
10. To work out the density of population in India, the entire area and population of those portions of Jammu and Kashmir that are under the illegal occupation of Pakistan and China have not been taken into account.

3

Urban India

In this chapter . . .

The population of any society lives in local communities. The larger the size of the population, the greater is the number of these communities. The communities also get classified in terms of the size of the population inhabiting them. The smaller communities are called villages, and the larger ones, towns and cities.[1] Since most of the people in the villages engage in agriculture and other related occupations, the population of these settlements is designated as rural to contrast with the urban population of the towns and cities. A distinction is also made between rural and tribal populations. Since the tribals also live in small communities and practise land-related economic activities, technically, the term 'rural' applies to them as well. What separates them is ethnicity and not the mode of residence. Of course, tribal communities characteristically lived in remote and difficult-to-reach villages and had little contact with the non-tribal villages and towns of their region. Development efforts made in independent India have changed the scenario. Through newly constructed roads and railway tracks, and through mass media of communication, these areas are also getting linked with other neighbourhood communities. As a result, what distinguishes them is not their place of residence, but their ethnic antecedents. Many tribal areas of the country, particularly in the Northeastern region have both rural and urban communities. Tribal groups are found to cohabit the same village as the non-tribal populations where they are treated as representatives of a separate caste.

In India, the population is divided into these three segments: urban, rural, and tribal. While the population of the first two categories is a mixed one and computed in terms of settlement, the tribal population is classified in terms of ethnic origin, as communities that inhabit a number of residential areas that are mostly rural. Micro-studies of the urban and rural communities are carried out in cities/towns or in villages, but ethnographic studies of the tribals – also called micro-cosmic studies – cover the entire tribe spread in a large number of adjacent settlements. In that sense, tribal ethnographies differ from the village studies, although the latter have also used anthropological techniques of field work.

According to the 2001 Census, 27.78 per cent of the Indian population lives in 3,947 towns and cities. There are 58,779 villages of different sizes, some of these overlap with the urban categories in terms of size. There are both urban and rural settlements that have populations of between 20,000 and 1,000. Villages of such large size number 76,291; cities and towns in this range are only 2,045. However, most villages have a population of less than 1,000; these number 3,90,093. The Table 1 gives the classification of villages and towns in terms of their size. The

Table 1
Distribution of Villages and Towns According to Population

Population	*Number of Urban Agglomerations and Towns*	*Percentage of Total Urban Population*	*Number of Villages*
100,000 and Above	296	65.2	
50,000-99,999	341	11.0	
20,000-49,999	927	13.2	
10,000-19,999	1,135	7.7	2,779
5,000-9999	725	2.6	10,597
1000-4999	185	0.3	62,915*
Total Towns	3,609	100.00	
1,000-1,999			1,14,395
Less than 1,000			3,90,093

* The class interval for the villages is 2,000-4,999.

figures for the villages are from the 1991 Census, and those for the towns and cities are from the 1981 Census.

In interpreting urbanization data, it should be kept in mind that the definition of what constitutes a 'town' has changed since the 1961 Census. Prior to that, the definition was rather loose and the Census superintendents were given the authority to use their discretion in determining the borderline cases. According to the 1901 Census, towns were defined to include:

(i) Every municipality of whatever size;
(ii) All civil lines not included within municipal limits; and
(iii) Every other continuous collection of houses, permanently inhabited by not less than 5,000 persons, and approved by the provincial superintendent as a town.

Thus, the primary consideration for classification of a settlement as urban was not the size, but the administrative set-up. That is why there were many towns that did not have even a population of 5,000; similarly, many overgrown villages, with a population of more than 5,000 people remained in the category of villages. In the 1951 Census, the definition was worded more concretely, though in essence, it did not differ much from the 1901 definition. The 1951 Census definition of a town was:

> A town is normally an inhabited locality with a total population of not less than 5,000 persons. But places with a somewhat larger population, which do not possess definite urban character, may not be treated as towns. At the same time, places with a smaller population with definite urban character (including generally all municipalities and cantonments and other places having a local administration of their own) may be treated as separate towns. The decision, in marginal cases, rests with state governments in some states and census superintendents in others.

However, the 1961 Census employed a more rigorous definition of town. It used four criteria:

(i) A density of not less than 1,000 per square mile;

(ii) A population of 5,000 and above;

(iii) Three-fourths of the occupations of the working population should be outside of agriculture; and

(iv) The place should have a few pronounced urban characteristics and amenities. The Census admitted that this criterion was vague, and would have scope for discretion on the part of the Census superintendent. But it 'was meant to cover newly founded industrial areas, large housing settlements, or places of tourist importance, which have been recently served with civil amenities'.

The application of these criteria not only included many new settlements in the urban category, but also eliminated a fair number of places that had earlier been classified as towns. As a result, there was a reduction in the number of towns between 1951 and 1961. Around 803 places from the 1951 Census were declassified and 54 were merged with other towns. This loss of 857 towns was compensated by the inclusion of 497 new towns, thus causing an overall deficit of 360. The total number came down from 3,060 in 1951 to 2,700 in 1961.

The 1971 Census used the same definition but replaced the term 'town group' with 'urban agglomeration', but the criteria remained the same. However, these criteria were uniformly applied in all the states.

A more clear-cut definition of what is an urban settlement is given in the 1991 Census. The same definition was followed in the 2001 Census. It included:

(a) Places with a municipality, corporation, cantonment board, notified town area committee; and
(b) Other places which satisfy the following criteria:
    — A minimum population of 5,000
    — At least 75 per cent of the male working population engaged in non-agricultural pursuits
    — A density of population of at least 400 persons per sq. km.

In addition, it also included major project colonies, areas of intensive industrial development, railway colonies, and important tourist centres. Thus, there are two types of towns: (i) those which have come into existence by virtue of statutory notification as municipal corporation, municipal board, cantonment board, or notified area committee, and (ii) those that satisfy the criteria laid down in (b) above. The latter are called Census towns (CTs), or non-municipal towns (NMTs).

An 'urban conglomeration' is defined as 'a continuous urban spread' that "normally consists of a town and its adjoining outgrowths, or two or more physically contiguous towns together with continuous well-recognized outgrowth, if any, of such towns". Examples of 'outgrowth' localities are railway colonies, university campuses, port areas, and military camps. These places are generally outside the statutory limits of a town, but fall within the boundaries of the adjoining village or villages.

As a result of the revised definition at the time of the 1991 Census, 93 towns were declassified, 103 towns were fully merged with other towns, and 856 new towns were added (of which 277 were statutory and 579, Census towns). In 1981, the number of towns and urban agglomerations was 3,245. The 1991 figures suggest that urban settlements numbered 3,609. These included the three mega cities[2] of Greater Mumbai, Kolkata, and Delhi. There are 23 cities with a population of more than a million, including the three mega cities. These cities are Chennai (5.42 million), Bangalore (4.1 million), Hyderabad (4.34 million), Ahmedabad (3.31 million), Kanpur (2.03 million), Pune (2.49 million), Nagpur (1.66 million), Lucknow (1.66 million), Jaipur (1.51 million), Surat (1.51 million), Kochi (1.14 million), Vadodara (1.12 million), Indore (1.11 million), Coimbatore (1.10 million), Patna (1.10 million), Madurai (1.08 million), Bhopal (1.06 million), Visakhapatnam (1.05 million), Ludhiana (1.04 million), and Varanasi (1.03 million). Together, the population of these places totalled 122.291 million in 1991. In 1951, India had only five cities that came in the million plus category. These were Calcutta (now renamed Kolkata), Greater Bombay (now renamed Vrihattar Mumbai), Delhi, Madras (now renamed Chennai), and Hyderabad. The 1961 and 1971 Censuses added two cities each to this list. In 1981, three more cities were added to this list. But the largest addition was in 1991, with 11 more cities falling into this category, bringing the total of million plus cities to 23.

At the time of the 2001 Census, there were 5,161 towns (including 502 statutory towns and 636 Census towns).

Table 2 compares the growth of urbanization by class of towns between 1901 and 1991.

Table 2

Growth of Urbanization by Class of Towns 1901-1991

(Population in '000s)

Class	Size	1901	1951	1961	1971	1981	1991
I	1,00,000 and Above	5,570	23,483	34,736	52,808	82,227	1,22,291 (296)
II	50,000-99,999	2,948	7,548	9,530	14,712	22,037	28,764 (341)
III	20,000-49,999	4,346	11,115	15,728	19,865	26,719	35,273 (927)
IV	10,000-19,999	5,847	9,331	11,241	13,929	17,588	21,079 (1135)
V	5,000-9,999	5,332	8,463	6,304	6,089	6,788	7,397 (725)
VI	Less than 5,000	1,650	2,047	805	853	1,062	967 (185)
	All Classes	25,693	61,987	78,343	1,08,256	1,56,420	2,15,772 (3609)
	Urban Population as Percentage to Total Population	10.84	17.29	19.97	19.91	23.34	25.72

It is estimated that in 1947, when the country became independent, the urban population constituted 15.7 per cent of its population, with 53 million people. In 2001, India's urban population stood at 285.35 million. During the period (1951-2001), there was only a marginal increase in the proportion of the urban population – from 17 per cent to 27.78 per cent. But this ten percentage point increase quadrupled the absolute numbers of those living in urban areas. Today, for every 100 people living in rural areas, 39 live in urban areas.

The refugees who fled from Pakistan in 1947 during partition, made a major contribution to the urban population; 54 per cent of the refugees settled in urban areas. Similarly, those who migrated to Pakistan were mainly from urban areas. The

Changing skyline in a metropolis

refugee migration accounted for 6.2 per cent of the 41 per cent increase in the urban population of India during the decade, 1941-51. It is important to mention that the rate of growth of urban population declined between 1981 and 2001 from 3.8 per cent to 2.08 per cent. Thus, while 58.1 million people were added to the urban population in 1971-81, in the following decade, only 50.4 million were added. In the last decade, 69.5 million people were added to this segment of the population. Of this number, the natural increase (births – deaths) was 59.98 per cent; another 22.62 per cent was due to net migration (immigration – migration); the remaining 17.40 per cent was the result of reclassification.

Analysing the decadal data, Ashish Bose says that between 1951 and 1961, "there was a marked shift in the distribution of towns by size class. It will be noted...that there was a significant increase in the number of towns with 10,000 population and over, and a considerable decrease in the number of towns with less than 10,000 people each...The proportion of total urban population living in towns with under 20,000 inhabitants declined from 32.0 per cent in 1951 to 23.4 per cent in 1961, while those living in towns with a population of 20,000 each showed an increase from 68.0 per cent to about 77 per cent." Here, it should be said that for purposes of international comparison, many scholars use a minimum of 20,000 persons as necessary for designating a place as urban. Using this criterion, the 1957 UN Report on the *World Social Situation* surveyed urbanization trends; these correspond to what has happened in India. To quote from the UN Report:

> Between 1800 and 1950, the population of the world living in cities with 20,000 or more inhabitants increased from about 21 million to 502.2 million, expanding 23 times in 150 years, while the total world population expanded about 2.6 times in the same period; 2.4 per cent of the world population lived in urban centres of 20,000 or more in 1800, 20.9 per cent in 1950 [p. 113].

As an aside, it should be said that urbanization is much faster in developing countries. The UN Report says: "Between 1900 and 1950, the population living in cities of 100,000 or more in Asia mounted from an estimated 19.4 million to 105.6 million (a gain of 444%), and in Africa from 1.4 million to 10.2 million (a gain of 629%)."

In the case of India, the urban population grew by 248 per cent between 1901 and 1951, and by 1,140 per cent between 1901 and 2001 – from 25 million in 1901 to 285 million in 2001. But this still constitutes only a little more than one-fourth of India's population. The main causes of urban growth are: the town being a capital city, growth of industries, a new industrial township, a new capital city, growth of agro-industries, a temple complex, a new university or educational complex, and annexation of adjoining areas (technically called the processes of 'conurbation' and 'suburbation'). Some projections suggest that by 2021, India will have 5,000 urban centres, inhabited by 618 million people (or 40% of the total population). This figure will almost be double of the total population of India in 1947! Furthermore, it is predicted that of the 5,000 and odd towns in 2021, there will be 70 towns with a population of more than a million people each, and another 500 towns with population ranging between a hundred thousand and a million. Despite the absolute increase in urban population in the future, the rate of growth of the urban population is expected to decline and stabilize at 3 per cent per annum. Most of this contribution will be through rural-urban migration.

The 2001 Census suggests that Maharashtra has the largest share of urban population in the country (14.4%), followed by Uttar Pradesh (12.1%) and Tamil Nadu (9.5%). If we add the urban population of West Bengal and Andhra Pradesh, then the total urban population in these five states would be nearly half of the all-India total. The states of Jammu and Kashmir and Assam have the lowest share of the urban population. One calculation suggests that the urban population of 17 states and Union territories together constitutes only 3.5 per cent of the total urban population. This is so because of the smaller size of these units. However, it should be said that each of the Union territories has a higher percentage of urban population as compared to the national average. One should, therefore, make a distinction between the demographic composition of a given state or Union territory (which may indicate the degree of its urbanization in terms of rural-urban ratio, for example) and its share in the country's total. To illustrate the point, Maharashtra tops in terms of its share in the country's urban population with 14.4 per cent, but the total urban population of Maharashtra is only 42.4 per cent; as against this, Delhi has a 93 per cent urban population, but it represents only 4.2 per cent of India's total urban population.

Typology of Urban Areas

Urban areas are a product of urbanization. Usually, urbanization is measured in terms of the size of the population living in urban areas, or the number of urban centres of different sizes. But those who regard urbanism as a 'way of life' use a different yardstick. They first define those characteristics that are 'urban' and inventorize their presence or absence in any given community to classify it as relatively more urban or less urban. This approach assumes that all communities are in a process of urbanization, moving from the rural end to the urban end, thus forming a rural-urban continuum. The concept of Census towns (CTs) is part of this way of looking at urbanization.

Various efforts have been made to classify towns, that is, to make a typology. One way of classifying towns is to see the auspices under which urbanization takes place. A natural urbanization, called 'indigenous' urbanization, can be contrasted with colonization under colonial rule and urbanization during the post-independence period as part of the developmental exercise. There are others who classify cities as 'pre-industrial', 'industrial', and 'metropolitan'. But all these attempts at classifying towns have their limitations because present-day cities are a mix of several functions. The older cities have taken new roles and even the new cities, created in the wake of industrialization, have adapted to traditional roles as well. The urban areas show different growth patterns. They also differ in the pattern of land use and their relationship with the rural hinterland.

Since there is no consensus on typology, we shall attempt to classify Indian cities according to different variables such as size, functions, and recency.

Size

The Census of India has classified cities in terms of their size into six categories:

Class	*Size*
I	100,000 and Above
II	50,000-99,999
III	20,000-49,999
IV	10,000-19,999
V	5,000-9,999
VI	Less than 5,000

Class I is further split into mega cities and million-plus cities. Mega cities are those that have a population of eight million or more. India has three mega cities – Greater Mumbai, Kolkata, and Delhi. There are 20 other cities that have more than a million population, but less than eight million. Thus, 23 cities fall into the first category.

Functions

Cities can be classified in terms of their predominant function such as religious place, capital city, trade centre, industrial township, port area, cantonment, academic complex (such as university town), etc. Some examples of each are given below:

Religious Places

These are also called temple towns. Important pilgrim centres are to be found in different parts of the country. Some of the older places have combined functions other than religious, while some have remained mainly religious centres, attracting pilgrims from all over the country. Among the old centres mention may be made of Varanasi, Allahabad, Ayodhya, Mathura, and Hardwar. Hindu pilgrims visit all these places. But these also have a substantial population of other religious groups. Varanasi and Allahabad are also important university towns.

Typical examples of temple towns are Tirupati in the South and Nathdwara in the North. The temples of Venkateshwar in Tirupati and of Shri Nathji in Nathdwara are visited by thousands of pilgrims every day. The temples shape the entire economy of these two townships. A large number of dharamshalas, eateries, souvenir shops, and temple guides and escorts distinguish these centres from other towns.

Capital Cities

These cities can be subclassified into the following four categories:

1. Former Capitals of Princely States: Udaipur, Jodhpur, Jaisalmer, Gwalior, Patiala
2. State Capitals (Old Townships): Lucknow, Jaipur, Bhopal
3. New Capital Towns: Chandigarh, Gandhinagar
4. New Status as a Capital: Dehradun (capital of Uttaranchal), Ranchi (capital of Jharkhand), and Raipur (capital of Chhatisgarh).

Trade Centres

Also called commercial towns, there are several of them. Some of these also serve as capitals of states, among them Mumbai and Kolkata. Many of such centres that are smaller in size are called Mandis.

Industrial Townships

Long before Ahmedabad became the capital of Gujarat, it was known as an industrial town; Now, the capital of Gujarat has moved to the new township of Gandhinagar, which is a twin city. Jamshedpur or Tatanagar is another example of such a town.

Twin Cities

To offload the overflowing population of big metropolitan cities, new townships have been planned adjacent to the big cities. That is how New (or *Navi)* Mumbai came into being. Gandhinagar, as the twin city of Ahmedabad, has been built to move the capital complex there. The National Capital Region (NCR) consists of those townships in the vicinity of the national capital, Delhi, which are now coming up in the adjoining states. Though such colonies are not called twin cities, they are functional equivalents of the twin-city concept, taking the overload of population from the city of Delhi. In fact, New Delhi is the oldest example of a twin city.

Other Functional Towns

In this category are included cantonments (Mhow,[3] Nasirabad), university towns (Pilani), and port cities (Visakhapatnam).

Recency

Cities can also be classified as ancient (Varanasi, Ujjain), mediaeval (Agra, Lucknow), colonial (Shimla, Mussoorie, Bangalore), and new townships (Chandigarh, Bhubaneswar).

Structure of the City

A city's structure can be described either in architectural terms or in terms of its social structure. In the case of India, it is indeed very difficult to make any generalizations about the cities because they vary in terms of their sites, situations, and degree of foreign influence. Gerald Breese, in his book, *Urbanization in Newly Developing Countries*, has, however, mentioned the following similarities in urban settlements in India:

(i) Combination of very high population density in relatively small areas and relatively low population density over other large areas – small area-high density and low density-large area contrast. In addition, burgeoning areas of temporary settlement at the periphery mark some large Indian urban areas. These are 'bustees' or 'tin-town' agglomerations;

(ii) Indian urban areas have contrasting road and circulation patterns. In the old areas, the roads and streets are narrow and confusing; in the new areas, the circulation is more diagonal;

(iii) "As in European cities, the railroads entered large urban areas at a relatively recent date. Consequently, they seldom penetrate the old city area, but thrust inward as far as possible to establish stations, goods yard, etc., then loop around … the built-up area;"

(iv) "The transportation 'mix' in large Indian urban areas further complicates circulation... Animal and vehicular transportation ranges from the sluggish camel and donkey to the speeding truck and the rapid commuter train... Between these are the tonga cart, pedicab, motorcycle rickshaw, bicycle, ox-cart, taxi and private automobile, trucks of various kinds, hand cart, bus …, to mention the chief modes of transportation", and

(v) There is highly mixed land use.

A 1983 survey of 407 towns and cities, carried out by the Town and Country Planning Organization, came out with the following findings with regard to land use:

(i) Proportion of developed land differs from one type of city to another. In the million-plus cities, it is 63 per

Emerging medium town

cent; in cities with population of between 100,000 and 500,000, developed land is 59 per cent, and in towns with less than 20,000 persons, it is only 22 per cent;

(ii) Residential land is 25 per cent of the total, but it is lowest (22%) in smaller size cities, and highest (40%) in larger size cities;

(iii) Only 2 to 3 per cent land is used for commercial purposes;

(iv) Industrial use accounts for 6.8 per cent of the developed land. It is 14 per cent in cities of larger size (more than half a million population);

(v) Parks and playgrounds occupy 2 to 5 per cent of the land;

(vi) 10.8 per cent land is kept for public use;

(vii) Roads and streets cover 10.9 per cent, and

(viii) 15.4 per cent is vacant land.

Social Structure of the City

Any settlement reflects the social structure of the society. The plurality of Indian society is also reflected in the cities of India. The cities have mixed populations, composed of different religious groups, including their internal differentiations such as castes or sects. The settlement pattern indicates the history of migrations – the old settlers living in the inner quarters and the newer ones on the outer. Also, the old cities reflect the social hierarchy, with higher castes in the centre or at the head, and the lower castes at the outer edges. Many of the old cities are divided into wards based on caste or religious group concentrations. Where occupational castes came to reside, the wards also became hubs of their economic activity. In many older cities, one can come across the wards of carpenters, ironsmiths, shoemakers, oil pressers, or basket makers. Since these cities grew on their own, without any conscious planning, their development is haphazard, and shows a mix of the old and the new.

With the arrival of the British, many cities added new features. One can talk of the indigenous city (or the old city), civil lines (*sadar*), cantonment area (*chhaavani*), special areas, bustees or slums, and village enclaves.

It is interesting to note that even the new townships that were fully planned have, in due course of time, become Indianized or localized. Take the case of Chandigarh, the joint capital of Haryana and Punjab. This city was built to be the new capital of Punjab as Lahore had gone to Pakistan. The state needed a capital town and a university campus. By acquiring land from several villages, the people of which were relocated or given compensation for relocation, a brand new township was planned by Le Corbusier to accommodate a population of half a million. It was divided into the capital complex, educational zone, the central zone for commerce and residence, and the industrial area. The entire township was divided into sectors, each sector with a residential area, a school, places for worship, parks and playgrounds, market for daily needs, and straight, connecting roads. The planners decided to locate different categories of people in different sectors to make them into socioeconomically homogeneous clusters.

Initially, the government found it difficult to attract buyers of land. The plots were sold at very nominal costs to government employees. But as the city started bustling with activity, land prices shot, and the owners modified the original plans and constructed additional floors to rent out portions to outsiders. Some hutments were also built for the much-needed domestic servants. The casual labour, which came from far-off places to work at construction sites, also built their thatched hutments. Over time, the sectors lost their homogeneity, land use patterns changed to reinvent tradition, and slum settlements grew. The original owners also saw merit in selling off their property in the main city at exorbitant prices and making a profit. These people moved to nearby villages and built their new houses there. Thus, two satellite towns have sprung up, one of which is in Haryana (Panchkula) and the other in Punjab (Mohali). It so happens that Mohali has a predominance of Sikhs, and Panchkula of the Hindu *Monas*. In all the three townships, several features of the older Indian towns have emerged. Thus, constructionwise, these appear to be modern, but culturally, they have assumed the character of Punjabi and Haryanvi towns.

Demographically, it is the towns that exhibit all the four processes of population growth, namely birth, death, immigration and emigration. For example, 8.38 million migrants are to be found in the 23 million-plus cities. In the first five cities – Mumbai, Kolkata, Delhi, Chennai, and Hyderabad – the migrants constitute around 57 per cent of the total migrants to the large cities. See Table 3.

We have studies of urban slums, beggary, prostitution, and of local-self government. While these problems continue to haunt our urban settlements, new problems are also cropping up as a

Table 3
Migrants in Five Major Cities

City	Total Migrants (Million)	% to the Total (N= 8.38 Million)	From Within State: Rural	From Within State: Urban	From Outside the State: Rural	From Outside the State: Urban	From Other Countries
Mumbai	1.54	18.13	30.5	14.9	35.0	18.1	1.2
Kolkata	0.71	8.55	35.2	18.8	20.7	10.3	15.0
Delhi	1.40	16.77	0.3	0.7	53.8	42.0	3.0
Chennai	0.58	6.94	33.4	42.6	5.5	16.3	1.6
Hyderabad	0.55	6.58	46.4	34.9	6.1	11.8	0.4

result of the expanding urban population. The processes of suburbation and conurbation are creating satellite towns that are taking over the land earlier utilized by the villages for purposes of agriculture. The new urban conglomerations require different strategies for their administration. For example, the metropolitan city of Delhi now has several satellite towns surrounding its borders, which touch the states of Haryana and Uttar Pradesh. This expanding region is called the National Capital Region (NCR). The cities of Noida and Ghaziabad in Uttar Pradesh and the cities of Faridabad and Gurgaon in Haryana are becoming virtually an extension of Delhi. The new colonies developing in these townships have changed their demography substantially, and influenced their economies remarkably. The big malls and multiplexes in these townships now attract people from the core city of Delhi. Both shoppers and employees working in the corporate sector and in the multinationals commute daily, causing problems of traffic congestion, pollution, theft and robbery. The new residents of the developing colonies have made these communities multi-cultural and modern. The old residents have become richer by selling their properties, leaving their traditional occupations and adopting a different lifestyle. The villages adjacent to the new colonies are now characterized by an urban way of life. Women, who were earlier working in the fields, have become domestic servants for the migrant affluent families. Men have also taken to new jobs and have renovated their living spaces to rent out portions to migrant labour, and also to adapt to the changing milieu. To meet the new demands, the government is now paying attention to improving the roads, and providing other civic amenities.

The visible affluence of the cities has, however, not eradicated urban poverty. One estimate suggests that there are nearly 1,100 slums (called Jhuggi-Jhonparis) in Delhi alone, where 39.45 per cent of the urban poor hailing from other parts of India and engaged in various types of jobs – from domestic servants, to masonry, daily wage labour, carpentry, plumbing, begging, rag-collection etc. – reside. It must be said that not all who live in these slums are poor. Skilled craftsmen and petty contractors and middlemen also rent these places. The same phenomenon can be seen in Gurgaon and Noida, where there is a rising number of workers in the housing construction industry. In Gurgaon, for example, people hailing from Bihar are generally engaged in masonry and unskilled labour related to construction. People from Orissa are found in jobs related to plumbing and electrical fittings. Thrown in are the allegedly illegal Bangladeshi migrants, who work as domestic servants and rikshaw pullers. All these reside in rented houses or temporarily built structures.

The slums are like temporary clusters of homes where no proper roads exist, electricity is scarce (and at times, illegally stolen), and there is no proper sanitation. When the city grows, the administration takes steps to remove the slums. But such slums crop up elsewhere to meet the demands of the migrant population for a roof over their heads. It is also seen that when land is provided to such dwellers by the government at concessional rates, the beneficiaries usually sell it to earn a profit rather than build a place for themselves. There is a growing feeling that slums should not be seen as illegal settlements or encroachments. Since the slum dwellers provide useful services to the urban rich of the same localities, they should be viewed as parts of a common social system. Some even go further to argue that the slums are productive clusters that significantly contribute to the urban economy. Therefore, efforts should be made to upgrade them, rather than uproot them. When slums arise in an unplanned manner, they indicate a lacuna in the planning process that fails to recognize their functional significance and allot a space for them.

The proliferation of slums is not merely a manifestation of poverty. It also indicates the growth of the informal sector and demands reconsideration of the policy towards urban development, including the provision of civic services.

In recent years, there is growing interest in urban sociology, primarily because of expanding urbanization. Despite this rising trend in urban studies, it is important to remember that in countries such as India, the size of the rural population is still very large. All of this cannot be accommodated in the existing cities and, therefore, we will have to do something to bring the cities to the villages, rather than take the villages to the cities. There is need to make improvements in our villages to withstand the pressures of increasing urbanization. Simultaneously, there is also a need to better understand our urban settlements and to improve their governance and social delivery systems. From the point of view of future studies the urban poor and the rural migrants to urban areas deserve our special attention. More importantly, there are illegal migrants from neighbouring countries in some of our cities. Besides, we have refugee populations such as Kashmiri Pandits and the Afghani families that reside in Delhi. The problems of their welfare and their resettlement pose special problems to the urban administration. Research on these topics should be given priority.

Most of the urban studies in India, carried out by sociologists, have focused on urban problems such as social disorganization, crime and violence, slums, migrant labour, and urban poor. Town planners, architects, and geographers have studied the towns from the planning and urban development angle. Various kinds of surveys have been carried out on urban samples. But these studies do not add up to give us a holistic picture of the city. There are very few studies of the social organization of the city. This is an area where research is badly needed.

Notes

1. That is why some scholars talk of urban villages. The prefix 'rural' or 'urban' specifies the character of these communities.
2. The United Nations define a mega city as any urban agglomeration that has eight million or more inhabitants. In 1970, there was no mega city in India. In 1990, Mumbai was included in the list. Now there are three: Mumbai (12.59 million), Kolkata (11.02 million), and Delhi (8.42 million).
3. Although people now take this name for granted, it is an abbreviation for the Military Headquarters of the Western Command. Some are of the view that the last letter of the acronym (W) stands for War. It is said that Sir John Malcolm founded it in 1818 as the headquarters of the Fifth Division of the Army after a treaty signed by the British with the Holkar kings of Indore.

4

Village India

In this chapter . . .

Mahatma Gandhi is often quoted as having said: "Real India lives in its villages." The fact that in the early decades of the 20th century, India's urban segment constituted only 11 per cent of the total population gave strength to his argument. It was the villages in which 89 per cent of the population lived. That made India an agricultural country. The development of Village India, for Gandhi, was the development of India. Illiteracy, ignorance, and poverty characterized the vast population of rural India. Gandhi organized mass movements to draw attention to the problems of the rural people, and also to involve the peasants in the freedom struggle. Social scientists also became interested in studying rural problems, particularly the deteriorating rural economy. The growing rural discontent also worried the British Government. It

A Gond farmer in a Madhya Pradesh village

felt the need to investigate the actually existing conditions. S.J. Patel, in his book *Agricultural Labourers in Modern India and Pakistan,*[1] talks about the growth of village studies:

> With the end of the First World War, the beginnings of an agrarian crisis was accompanied by the entry of peasants into the political arena, as exemplified during the Champaran and Kaira campaigns led by Gandhiji. As a result, the cultivator of the soil began to attract considerable attention from students of Indian society. G. Keatings and Harold Mann in Bombay, Gilbert Slater in Madras, and E.V. Lucas in the Punjab initiated intensive studies of particular villages and general agricultural problems. The results of these investigations evoked great interest and stressed the necessity for still further study [1952: 1].

Economists and social anthropologists later joined the movement of village studies. In the 1950s, several studies of individual villages were undertaken. In 1955, four major publications came out, three of which were anthologies of articles written by social anthropologists/sociologists on the villages studied by them, and the fourth one was a full-length monograph – the very first and by an Indian social scientist. The anthologies were *Rural Profiles* (edited by D.N. Majumdar), *India's Villages* (edited by M.N. Srinivas), and *Village India* (edited by Mckim Marriott). S.C. Dube authored the full-length monograph on a village in Andhra Pradesh under the title, *Indian Village*. With the arrival of these publications, a new trend of village studies was ushered in Indian sociology.

These studies shattered the stereotypical images of the Indian village, and also provided accounts of the caste system as it obtains now, different from the prevailing book view and the upper caste view.

In the past, many scholars had painted an idyllic picture of the village. People believed what Sir Charles Metcalfe, a British administrator, once wrote about the village communities of India. This is what he said:

> The Village Communities are little republics, having nearly everything that they want within themselves and almost independent of any foreign relations. They seem to last where nothing else lasts. Dynasty after dynasty tumbles down; revolution succeeds to revolution, Hindoo, Pathan, Mogul, Mahratta, Sikh, English, are all masters in turn; but the Village Communities remain the same.

Such a description of the village community in India was idyllic and superficial. Although villages had their distinct identity and were ruled by the local heads, they could not be called 'republics'. Villages were remote and relatively cut off from each other, but they were never isolated, having nothing to do with the outside world. They were part of the Great Tradition of India, having various links with the people living in other places. They also had affiliations with the regional states that ruled them and provided them protection. Being illiterate and attached to their land, the villagers led a simple life.

Villages in Ancient India

There is sufficient evidence to suggest that the village was one of the important settlements in ancient India. The *Rig Veda* talks about the *gram* to which various families owed their allegiance. Valmiki's *Ramayana* talks of two types of villages – the *ghosh* and the *gram*. The *ghosh* was smaller than the gram and was also known as *vraja, or brij* (signifying a cattle farm). Both types of villages had their officials, called the *mahattar*. There is also a reference to a senior official called *gramani* or *gramik*. The Mahabharat talks of different types of settlements, for example, *ghosh* or *brij* (cattle farm), *palli* (small hutments), *gram* (villages around the forts or *durgs*), *kharvata* or *pattan* (towns), and *pur, puri, nagar* (cities of different types). The villages were linked with one another, culturally, socially and administratively. The administrator of ten villages was called *dashi*; of 20 villages, *vinshati;* of 100 villages, *shati*; and of over 1,000 villages, *sahasra gramadhipati*. This is a clear indication of the interlinkages between the villages.

Kautilya's *Arthashastra* suggests that river, hill, forests, ditches, tanks, bunds or trees demarcated village boundaries. He prescribed that villages should be situated at distances of one or two *krosha* (in Rajasthan, it is spelt as *koss,* which is the equivalent of two miles or 3.219 km) from each other so that in times of need, one village could go to the help of the other. The villages were organized thus:

10 villages	*Samgrahana*
200 villages	*Karvatika*
400 villages	*Dronamukha*
800 villages	*Mahagrama* or *Sthatnuja*[2]

During the period of Chandragupta Maurya, the villages were divided into three categories according to their size: *Jyeshtha* (the biggest), *Madhyama* (medium sized) and *Kanishtha* (smaller ones). In terms of land revenue, these villages were put into four categories:

Gramagra	Ordinary villages paying tax in cash
Pariharak	Revenue free, given to priests and teachers, who would collect the tax from the villagers and use it as their salary for spreading education and pursuing a religious life
Ayudhuja	Revenue free, for supplying soldiers during a war
Anya	Villages allowed to pay tax in kind in the form of agricultural products, minerals or labour

The villages have remained the administrative units of various princely states. The maharajas or maharanas appointed *jagirdars* or zamindars and collected revenues, called *lagaan*, through them. The practice of giving a village to a priest or not charging any *lagaan* from an agriculturist family continued until recently. In Rajasthan, such lands or villages were called *Mafi ki Zameen* or *Mafi ke Gaon*.

Villages Today

There were 580,781 villages in India, according to the 1991 Census.[3] Of these, the largest number (390,093) consisted of small-sized villages with a population of less than 1,000. In the category of 1,000-2,000 population are another 114,395 villages. Taken together, they represent 86 per cent of the villages of India. Villages with 2,000-5,000 population total 62,915, and those having a population of between 5,000-10,000 number 10,597. The highest concentration of very large villages, with more than 10,000 people, is to be found in the state of Kerala, which has 1,007 (of the 2,779) large villages.

At the time of the 2001 Census, the number of villages had gone up to 638,691. Like the 1991 Census, Uttar Pradesh (UP) continues to have the largest number of villages, although the state has become somewhat smaller with the state of Uttaranchal carved out of it. UP has 107,452 villages and Uttaranchal, 16,823, making a combined total of 124,275. While data exist for the average size of the village in each state in 2001, the, distribution of villages in different sizes is not yet available. On that basis, however, it can be said that the average size of villages in different states of India range between 17,281 (in Kerala) and 214 (in Arunachal Pradesh). In Uttar Pradesh, the average size of the village is 1,224 people, while in Uttaranchal, it is 375. Table 1 gives the distribution of villages according to population, based on the 1991 Census.

The table clearly indicates that the largest number of villages is in the state of Uttar Pradesh, followed by Madhya Pradesh and Bihar. All the three states are now smaller with the creation of the new states of Uttaranchal, Chhatisgarh, and Jharkhand, respectively. But this partition of the state territories does not affect their position in terms of their large rural population and rural settlements. It is interesting that most of the villages in the state of Kerala are in the category of large villages. The state has 1,384 villages, of which 1,007 are big villages with more than 10,000 people each. It has only seven villages that are below the size of 1,000 people.

It is obvious that the number of villages in a given state is dependent upon the size of the state and the proportion of population dependent on agriculture. In this context, it will be

Returing from the farms

Village hutments

Table 1

Distribution of Villages According to Population Size, 1991

S. No.	*States/ UTs*	*Less Than 1,000*	*1,000 to 1,999*	*2,000 to 4,999*	*5,000 to 9,999*	*10,000 and More*	*Total*
1	*2*	*3*	*4*	*5*	*6*	*7*	*8*
	India	390,093	114,395	62,915	10,597	2,779	580,781
1.	Uttar Pradesh	74,866	24,523	11,949	1,336	129	112,803
2.	Madhya Pradesh	56,568	11,426	3,264	261	7	71,526
3.	Bihar	45,164	12,768	7,647	1,604	330	67,513
4.	Orissa	39,309	5,761	1,812	103	4	46,989
5.	Maharashtra	24,111	10,632	4,715	762	192	40,412
6.	West Bengal	22,701	8,065	5,819	1,117	208	37,910
7.	Rajasthan	27,123	7,060	3,255	420	31	37,889
8.	Karnataka	17,113	5,861	3,422	570	100	27,066
9.	Andhra Pradesh	11,856	6,433	6,510	1,474	313	26,586
10.	Assam	17,784	4,988	1,793	111	9	24,685
11.	Gujarat	8,528	5,432	3,418	575	75	18,028
12.	Himachal Pradesh	16,361	495	136	5	-	16,997
13.	Tamil Nadu	4,915	4,625	4,764	1,247	271	15,822
14.	Punjab	7,447	3,130	1,628	209	14	12,428
15.	Haryana	2,627	2,021	1,703	364	44	6,759
16.	Meghalaya	5,316	129	38	1	-	5,484
17.	Arunachal Pradesh	3,538	82	25	3	1	3,649
18.	Manipur	1,834	192	135	16	3	2,182
19.	Kerala	7	16	102	252	1,007	1,384
20.	Nagaland	929	170	108	8	1	1,216
21.	Tripura	195	203	348	94	15	855
22.	Mizoram	616	61	19	2	-	698
23.	A&N Islands	445	44	15	-	-	504
24.	Sikkim	336	79	29	3	-	447
25.	Goa	156	78	94	31	1	360
26.	Pondicherry	174	48	38	3	-	263
27.	Delhi	29	44	86	19	21	199
28.	D&N Haveli	27	17	25	1	1	71
29.	Chandigarh	7	6	8	3	1	25
30.	Daman and Diu	9	6	6	2	1	24
31.	Lakshadweep	2	-	4	1	-	7

useful to understand two concepts, namely that of 'agricultural crowding' and 'village group'.

Agricultural crowding means the number of persons dependent on agriculture per square mile of cultivated land. In India, the average agricultural crowding was 432 in 1931; it rose to 535 in 1941, when it was greatest in Bengal (769) and least in Bombay Province (186). This difference coincides with the geography of the area. In dry or hilly areas, agricultural crowding is expected to be the least as compared to plain areas, where there is extensive agriculture.

The Census of India, 1951, developed the concept of the village group. It divided the entire territory of India into squares of five miles into five miles (an area of 25 sq. miles), numbering 47,074 squares. All villages falling in a given square were called a village group. Putting the 5,58,089 Census villages at that time into these squares, the 1951 Census came to the conclusion that, on an average, each village group consists of a dozen villages, each with around 500 inhabitants. The distribution of village groups in different zones of India in 1951 is given below:

Table 2
Village Groups in Different Zones (1951)

Zone	*Average Number of Villagers per Village*	*Villages and Villagers in an Average Village Group*	
		Number of Villages	*Number of Villagers (in 000s)*
North India	489	25	12.2
East India	433	18	7.8
South India	1,052	9	9.0
West India	708	7	5.0
Central India	431	9	3.9
Northwest India	447	8	3.6
India	529	12	6.3

These figures give an idea of the size of villages both in terms of area occupied and the population that inhabits it. Because the average size of the village is smaller in North India, the number of villages in this zone is much larger as compared to the South. This point will become further clear if we compared the distribution of villages of different sizes in various zones. The data are from the 1951 Census, but they hold good for this purpose.

Table 3

Variation in Size Pattern of Villages between Different Zones (1951)

Zone	*Percentage of Rural Population Living in*			
	Small Villages (under 500)	*Medium Sized (500-2,000)*	*Large Villages (2,000-5,000)*	*Very Large Villages (over 5,000)*
North India	29.8	55.3	13.5	1.4
East India	33.8	48.6	14.3	3.3
South India	9.4	38.5	35.3	16.8
West India	18.1	55.0	23.9	3.0
Central India	35.7	50.4	13.0	0.9
Northwest India	30.4	50.9	16.4	2.3
India	26.5	48.8	19.4	5.3

The villages in India do not differ only in terms of size. They also differ in terms of their physical structure. Irawati Karve[4] identified three main types of villages in Maharashtra. These are:

1. Tightly Nucleated Villages (with the habitation clearly defined from the surrounding cultivated fields): "In such villages, while the habitation area is well marked, the boundaries of the village, together with its fields,

are never perceived. The fields owned by one village merge into those owned by another, except where a hillock or a stream or a highway forms the boundary".

2. Coastal Villages: Found in the Konkan area, the "villages are generally strung along lengthwise on the two sides of a road. The houses stand in their own compounds with their fruit and coconut gardens and fenced on all sides... There are numerous tiny streams joining the Arabian Sea and there are also spurs of the Western mountains (the Sahyadri) coming right into the ocean... These natural obstacles divide one village from the other. Where these are absent, one village merges into the other and a casual traveller does not become aware of having crossed from one habitat area into another...In such villages, the exploitation of land is of two types – horticulture and agriculture... There is no sharp distinction between the habitation area and the cultivated area."
3. Dispersed Villages: These are found in the Satpura Mountains on the Northwestern boundary of the Marathi-speaking region. "The houses are situated in their own fields in clusters of two or three huts, all belonging to a single, close kinship group... The next cluster of huts may be as far as a furlong or two away, depending on how big the holding of each cluster is. The village boundaries are many times not defined by streams or hillocks because the houses belonging to one village are situated on separate hillocks or divided by streamlets".

Shantibhushan Nandi and D.S. Tyagi[5] have provided another classification of the villages. They have suggested four distinct types:

1. Shapeless Cluster or agglomerate with streets not forming an integral part of the design. These may be of the massive or dispersed type, in which the village is

reckoned to consist of an assemblage of discrete, small-sized clusters.

2. Linear Cluster, or assemblage, with a regular open space or straight street provided between parallel rows of houses.
3. Square or Rectangular Cluster, with straight streets running parallel or at right angles to one another.
4. Villages formed of Isolated Homesteads, a number of which are treated together as a *mauza* for convenience of collecting rents or taxes.

It is also possible to classify villages as tribal villages, single-caste villages, and multi-caste villages, or mixed villages (having populations of different religions also). Corresponding to type 4 in the above classification are the villages of the tribal Bhils in Mewar (part of Rajasthan). G. Morris Carstairs describes these settlements thus:

> Villages in this Bhil country are quite unlike those of the plains. Bhil houses are built at some distance from each other. Sometimes a man's married sons will build their homes close to their father's, but most houses are alone, built strategically on the top of the small hill, or on a jungle slope, so as to command a view over the paths of approach. To a stranger, these houses seem to be scattered at random all over the countryside, but stop and speak to any Bhil and he will be able to say to which village his house belongs, and who is his *Mukhi* or headman....
>
> To a newcomer, a striking feature about these northern Bhils is that they all go about armed, carrying bows and arrows, or muskets or swords – and, invariably, a sharp dagger in a sheath at their waists. When they see a stranger walking in their hills, they stand with weapons at the ready, looking to see who he is; and this wariness is

> not misplaced because robbery and violence are of common occurrence. At night, they sleep huddled round a log fire, on the earth floor of their flimsy leaf and bamboo huts, and they sleep with one eye open, ready to rush to the attack if a raider tries to steal one of their cattle in the dark. When this happens, they cry 'thief', and someone runs to beat the drum, which is kept in every *Mukhi*'s house. This brings out all men of the village armed and ready for a fight.[6]

From the point of view of land revenue, the villages in India were classified as the 'joint' or the 'severalty' (or *Ryotwari)*. The first type is found mostly in Northern India and the second type in Central and Peninsular India as well as in Bengal and Bihar prior to 1793, when the Permanent Settlement took place there.

The joint villages are further subdivided into *Pattidari* and *Zamindari*.

Pattidari is derived from the word *patta*, an official registration document that was issued to a joint family, which constituted a proprietary body to own separate shares in cultivable land and other pasture grounds.

In the *zamindari* system, all the land of the village was held in common and the tenants paid their rent to a common fund from which the common expenses were met. The zamindars were local agents serving as an intermediary between the government and the peasants. It was their duty to deposit fixed revenue at a fixed time to the government.

The *Ryotwari* or *Raiyatwari* system was set up by the British to do away with the intermediaries and make direct settlement with the actual cultivators. It can be regarded as the beginning of the registration system. In a *Ryotwari* village, the unit for land revenue was the individual landholder and not the village as a whole. The village did not have any waste land in common, though villagers used unoccupied land for grazing and for collecting fuelwood.

Whatever the type of settlement, either in terms of its physical structure or the structure of revenue and administration, the village is an easily identifiable unit. It is remarkable that the Indian postal system reached every village, Categorized in terms of its location in the *tehsil*, district, and state. Over the years, the villages have also been linked through roads and railways. There are only a few villages that are difficult to reach because of their remote location or difficult terrain.

In earlier times, villages were a little more isolated and communications on a day-to-day basis existed only in a limited area. Only on important events – such as marriages or deaths – did people from distant places visit the village. In those times, most of the villages were small, making it possible for all the resident families to know each other. Usually, a village consisted of people of different castes, each caste represented by a few inter-related families. In North India, the smaller villages followed exogamy, or not allowing marriages within the village; as a result, each village got linked with a number of other villages through affinal relations. In the South, where marriages between cross cousins and also between mother's brother and sister's daughter are generally preferred, villages do not practise exogamy.

The village can be regarded as a vertical unity of castes. Families belonging to different castes of the Hindu *varna*[7] constituted the social system of the village. The key distinction between them was occupation. Hereditarily fixed occupations combined with endogamy and rules of commensality arranged these castes in a hierarchical order in the *varna* scheme. The caste provided a social foundation to the village community and became a distinguishing feature of the Indian village. However, it must be said that other groups not belonging to the Hindu fold, but living in the same habitat, were also treated as functional equivalents of caste. The Muslims and the tribal families living in the villages maintained their separate identities as 'non-Hindu' castes because of endogamy and their occupational differentiation. It should also be noted that all occupations in the village were/and are not caste based. There are open occupations as well. Only caste linked occupations were practised by the people of a given caste and passed on from one generation to another. In terms of power structure, landholdings played an important role. Landless labourers were subordinate to the landowners. The artisan castes constituted a separate segment.

The village is not only a physical unity, but also a social and ritual unity. People of the village pay due regard to all the village deities. In North India, for example, there is always a foundation deity installed at the time of the founding of the village. In Rajasthan, at the outskirts of a village are the deities of pilgrimage called *Pathwari,* which are worshipped when people go for long-distance pilgrimages. The returnees also rest there until the villagers arrive to receive them and take them to the village in a procession.

The village is also an economic unity in the sense that families depend on each other. The artisan castes serve the agricultural castes; the Brahmin priest officiates at the religious ceremonies and also on important events in an individual's life cycle. Payments for services are usually made in kind. This system in the North was better known as the *Jajmani* system.

As a political unity, the village is both an administrative unit as well as a community with its headman and a village council called the Panchayat. Alongside informal Panchayats, the government has introduced the system of Panchayati Raj, as part of the process of democratic decentralization. The government official at the village level is the *patwari,* a settlement official who keeps records and maps of the land. Village Panchayats are linked with district councils (Zila Parishads) and are serviced by the district administration. With the provision of reservation of seats in the Panchayats for the scheduled castes, scheduled tribes and women, the Panchayats now differ greatly from the traditional village Panchayats, which were dominated by the people of the powerful castes. This has brought about radical change in village governance.

All this goes to show that the village is not an insulated entity. Within the village, different caste groups are vertically arranged, forming a sort of hierarchy. They are interdependent. But each individual caste group has its membership, extending to a large number of villages. Since the defining characteristic of the caste is its endogamy, the range of marital ties demarcates the effective area of caste interaction. In this sense, caste membership provides an outlet to get linked to an area wider than the village of one's residence. Like the village, castes also have their own Panchayats, which take decisions against their erring members. These cases relate to eating tabooed food, marrying outside the caste, widow remarriage, elopement, etc. The villages are also linked through religion to the wider Indian society. Villagers visit places of worship, pilgrimage centres; similarly, saints, sadhus and Brahmin priests from other places visit different villages. Administrative offices, courts, marketplaces, and fairs and exhibitions take the villagers to other destinations. Now, young children are also sent to big villages or nearby towns for schooling. Villagers go to towns for medical treatment in hospitals. Many villagers have moved to towns for work. Their return for family holidays brings with them many ideas and elements of the outside world.

This situation is not new. M.N. Srinivas wrote the following about the villages way back in 1955:

> The villager's social field is thus much wider than his village. Kin, economic, religious and other social ties enlarge the field to include a circle of neighbouring villages. But ever since the beginning of British rule, political and economic decisions taken in London and

> Manchester have affected the Indian peasant in his remotest villages. And in Independent India, not a day passes without some fresh evidence of government's solicitude for the rural folk. The social anthropologist who studies a single village should not only bear in mind its ties with other villages, but also that political and economic forces set in motion in large society affect it fundamentally.[8]

The Indian village is in the throes of change. Even the anthropological descriptions of the villages of the 1950s and 1960s are now dated. Take literacy, for example. In 1961, rural literacy was as low as 22.46 per cent as compared to urban literacy, which was 54.43 per cent. Census 2001 figures indicate that rural literacy now stands at 59.21 per cent, more than the urban percentage for 1961; in terms of actual numbers, the size of rural literates is considerable. Similarly, there is better connectivity in terms of roads and transport. The reach of the mass media has also considerably enlarged. All this has broken the isolation of the villages and created several spheres of interactions between the rural and the urban. The time has come to once again return to the villages and draw the contours of change in them afresh.

Notes

1. Published by Current Book House, Mumbai, in 1952.
2. The word *thana,* used today for a police station, might have been derived from this word, or from *sthana* (place).
3. These figures exclude Jammu & Kashmir.
4. See Irawati Karve, 'The Indian Village', in A.R. Desai's *Rural Sociology in India*, 1969, 4th Edition, Popular Prakashan, Mumbai, pp. 186-192. It is reproduced from the *Deccan Bulletin*, Vol. XVIII.

5. See their chapter titled 'Forms of Villages', in A.R. Desai (ed.), *Rural Sociology in India*, 1969, 4th Revised Edition, Popular Prakashan, Mumbai, pp. 206-217.
6. In *India's Villages,* edited by M.N. Srinivas, West Bengal Government Press, 1955, pp. 63-64.
7. We shall discuss caste in a separate chapter.
8. M.N. Srinivas, *India's Villages*, 1955, p. 10.

5

Tribal India

In this chapter . . .

India has a rich and varied tribal heritage. Not only are the various tribal communities scattered all over India, they also represent different racial and linguistic stocks and are at different levels of economic and technological development. While several changes have occurred amongst them with the spread of education and other programmes of development initiated by the government of independent India, most of these groups are still generally backward and receive special attention from the government and other social reform agencies. These tribal groups, called *Vanvasis, Adivasi, and Janjatis* are technically autochthonous people. Anthropologists study them as 'primitive cultures'. These groups differ from each other, and from the non-tribals, in matters of dress, customs, traditions, world-view, religion, and social structure. The distinct identity of these cultures is maintained even today because of their relative isolation. Where such isolation has broken, the tribal traits have intermingled with the evolving Great Tradition of India; simultaneously, the tribal societies have also absorbed several outside traits. Today's tribal India is very different from the colonial times; waves of change have reached them and broken their isolation in several ways.

The contemporary tribal cultures of India, thus, do not conform to the ideal of a primitive culture. Their settlements are both rural and urban; the rates of literacy among them are rising. Of course, some tribal groups, or some segments among them, still practise primitive economy and their ways of life correspond to the stereotypical image, but there are others that are on the path to modernization. Such changes notwithstanding, all tribal societies listed in the Schedule insist on maintaining their tribal status. They are designated as Scheduled Tribes (STs).

The tribal cultures provide us with some clues of the cultural raw materials that contributed to the development of Indian civilization. Their peculiar socio-cultural adjustment with the rest of Indian society helps us understand the emergence of the Great Tradition of India, namely, the indigenous Indian civilization.

Who are the tribals? Because of a continuous culture contact with the non-tribal communities surrounding them, it becomes difficult at times to isolate them. Where the representatives of these groups have settled in villages with other groups, they have been accorded the status of a caste, and they interact in the caste system of the village.[1] This has created difficulties in defining the tribe separately from the caste. In the Indian context, the term, tribe, has been used very loosely for denoting different kinds of groups. Some use it for the groups that are the 'original inhabitants' of India living before the 'advent' of Aryans, but some writers have called even the Aryan tribal groups. Similarly, Jats and Rajputs are also called tribals.

S.C. Dube has listed the following characteristics of a tribal group, though it is not necessary for any tribal group to possess all of them:

1. Their roots in the soil date back to a very early period. If they are not original inhabitants, they are at least among the oldest inhabitants of the land. Their position, however, cannot be compared to that of the Australian aborigines or American Indians, or native Africans. The Kols and Kirda of India had a long association with later immigrants. Mythology and history bear testimony to their encounters and intermingling;
2. They live in the relative isolation of the hills and forests. This was not always so. There is evidence of their presence in the *panchanad* and the Gangetic Valley;
3. Their sense of history is shallow for, among them, the remembered history of five to six generations tends to get merged in mythology. Some tribes have their own genealogists, with interesting anecdotes and remembered history;
4. They have a low level of techno-economic development;
5. In terms of their cultural ethos – language, institutions, beliefs, world-view, and customs – they stand out from the other sections of society; and
6. If they are not egalitarian, they are by and large at least non-hierarchic and undifferentiated. There are some exceptions: Some tribes have had ruling aristocracies; others have landed gentry.[2]

Concerned with the relative backwardness of the tribal population, the Constitution makers decided to grant special privileges to them. For this purpose, the Constitution recommended preparation of a Schedule listing all the tribal groups that would qualify for such special treatment. Article 342 (1) of the Constitution of India reads thus:

> The President may with respect to any State or Union territory, and where it is a State, after consultation with the Governor on ...thereof, by public notification, specify the tribes or tribal communities or parts of or groups within tribes or tribal communities which shall for the purposes of this Constitution be deemed to be Scheduled Tribes in relation to that State or Union territory, as the case may be.

Article 342 (2) further says:

> Parliament may by law include in or exclude from the list of Scheduled Tribes specified in a notification issued under clause (1) any tribe or tribal community or part of or group within any tribe or tribal community, but save as aforesaid a notification issued under the said clause shall not be varied by any subsequent notification.

To assist the President of India in notifying the groups as scheduled tribes, in accordance with the provision of the Constitution, the Backward Classes Commission, set up in January 1953, laid down the following criteria:

> They live apart in hills, and even when they live in plains, they lead a separate excluded existence and are not assimilated in the main body of the people. Scheduled Tribes may belong to any religion. They are listed as Scheduled Tribes because of the kind of life led by them.

The Census of India, 1951, listed 212 groups as scheduled tribes. Later, many more tribes were added, taking the total number to 571.

It must be said here that it was not easy to identify all the groups that qualified for inclusion in the Schedule. The Chairman of the Scheduled Areas and Scheduled Tribes Commission (known as the Dhebar Commission, because it was headed by U.N. Dhebar) wrote in his submission to the President of India (in 1961) about "the anomaly that existed in the preparation of the list of Scheduled Tribes. The old State of Hyderabad did not recognize the Yenadis, Yerukulas, and Sugalis as Scheduled Tribes, whereas the old Andhra State recognized them as such and with abundant justification. Similar is the case of the Gaddis who are found in Himachal Pradesh and the adjoining Punjab Hills. In Himachal Pradesh, they are recognized as Scheduled Tribes, but in the Punjab, they are treated as Scheduled Tribes only in the scheduled areas where they do not live." Similarly, the state of Uttar Pradesh did not recognize the Khasa of Jaunsar-Bawar and the Gonds and the Cheros of Mirzapur district as tribes. These anomalies went on rising as the years passed. For example, the Gujjars, Kinnaura and the Lauhola are included in the Schedule for Himachal Pradesh, but not in Jammu & Kashmir.

Geographical Distribution

The tribal population in India is dispersed all over the country, though there are some pockets of their concentration. There are in all 571 tribes included in the Schedule. Of these, 108 tribes are to be found in the Northeastern region, 28 in the Northwestern region, 176 in Central India, 95 in Western India, 143 in the South, and 12 in different islands.

The North and Northeastern zone harbours tribes like the Garo, Khasi, Naga, Bhotia, Tharu, Lauholese, Lepcha, Gaddi, Dafla, Abor-Miri, Mikir, and the Gurung.

A former head-hunter of Tirap decorates his basket with a plastic doll instead of the traditional carved wooden head

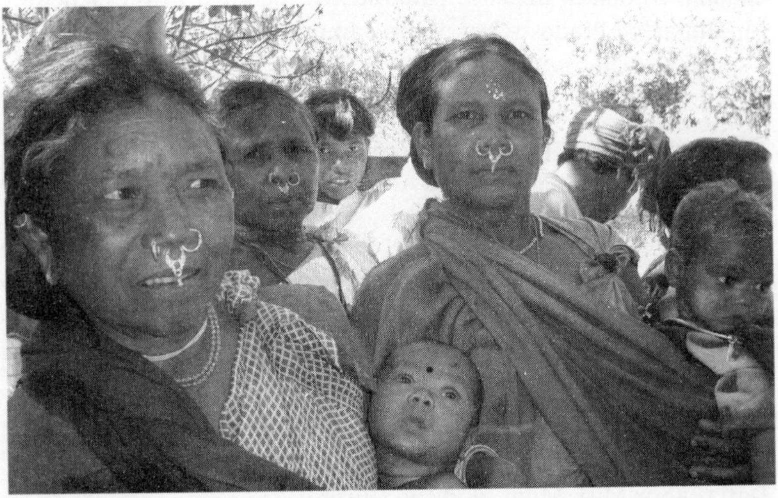

Kodhu women

The Central zone of India has a major concentration of tribals covering the states of West Bengal, Bihar, Orissa, Madhya Pradesh, Southern Uttar Pradesh, and Maharashtra (the Vidarbh area). Some of the important tribes of this zone are the Munda, Ho, Oraon, Maria and Muria Gonds, Kamar, Chaukhuntia-Bhunjia, Santals, Birhor, Bondo, Juang, and the Khond.

The Western zone, comprising Rajasthan, Gujarat, and parts of Maharashtra, has tribals such as the Bhil, Meena, Mahadeo Hill Koli, Garasia, and the Warli.

The area south of the Vindhyas (below Latitude 16) – the Southern zone – has a large number of small tribal communities. Here, the concentration is found in the southernmost part of the Western Ghats, stretching from Wynaad to Cape Comorin. Scholars believe that these people are the most ancient inhabitants of India who were pushed to these relatively remote habitats by the intruding groups of relatively more advanced cultures. Among these groups are included the Chenchu, Yuruva, Irula, Paniyan, Kurumba, Malapantaram, Toda, Kota, Kadar, and the Badaga.

Besides these, the Andaman and Nicobar Islands in the Bay of Bengal are home to the Jarawa, Onge, North Sentinelese, and the Nicobarese.

In the undivided India of 1941, the tribal population constituted 7.8 per cent (24,712,000) of the total Indian population. Because of the partition of the country in 1947, the 1951 Census recorded their population at 19,116,498, which was 5.36 per cent of the total. This shortfall was due both to the factor of partition (which took away some of the tribals of the North-West Frontier Province, which went to Pakistan, and some tribal groups of East Bengal, which is now Bangladesh) and the reclassification of some tribal groups as castes. In the 1991 Census, the population of the tribals stood at 67,758,000, an increase of 48 million from the 1951 figure, representing 8.08 per cent of the population. Table 1

Table 1

Population of Scheduled Tribes by States and Union Territories 1991

S. No.	India/State or UT	Population (000s)	Percentage of Total Population
	India	**67,758**	**8.08**
	States		
1.	Andhra Pradesh	4,199	6.31
2.	Arunachal Pradesh	550	63.66
3.	Assam	2,874	12.82
4.	Bihar	6,617	7.66
5.	Goa	-	0.03
6.	Gujarat	6,162	14.92
7.	Haryana	-	-
8.	Himachal Pradesh	218	4.22
9.	Karnataka	1,916	4.26
10.	Kerala	321	1.10
11.	Madhya Pradesh	15,399	23.27
12.	Maharashtra	7,318	9.27
13.	Manipur	632	34.41
14.	Meghalaya	1,518	85.53
15.	Mizoram	654	94.75
16.	Nagaland	1,061	87.70
17.	Orissa	7,032	22.21
18.	Punjab	-	-
19.	Rajasthan	5,475	12.44
20.	Sikkim	91	22.36
21	Tamil Nadu	574	1.03
22.	Tripura	853	30.95
23.	Uttar Pradesh	288	0.21
24.	West Bengal	3,809	5.60
	Union Territories		
1.	Andaman & Nicobar Islands	27	9.54
2.	Chandigarh	-	-
3.	Dadra & Nagar Haveli	109	78.99
4.	Daman and Diu	12	11.54
5.	Delhi	-	-
6.	Lakshadweep	48	93.15
7.	Pondicherry	-	-

gives the breakdown of the tribal population by states and Union territories in 1991.

The table can be interpreted in two ways: in terms of the absolute number of people belonging to the tribal category, and in terms of the proportion of tribals in the total population of the state. In absolute numbers, the highest concentration is to be found in Madhya Pradesh, with a total tribal population of more than 15 million, though it constitutes only 23.27 per cent of the state's total population. Other states with large tribal populations are Maharashtra and Orissa (seven million each), Bihar and Gujarat (with more than six million), and Rajasthan (5.4 million). Other states that have more than a million tribals are Andhra Pradesh (4.1 million), West Bengal (3.8 million), Assam (2.87 million), Karnataka (1.91 million), Meghalaya (1.5 million), and Nagaland (1.06 million). Chandigarh, Delhi, Haryana, Pondicherry, and Punjab have no tribal population.

But the picture in terms of proportion of tribal population in the state is quite different. While larger absolute numbers are related to the size of the state or the Union territory, the

Table 2

Percentage Distribution of Tribal Groups in Various Regions

60% and Above	Mizoram (94.75), Lakshadweep (93.15), Nagaland (87.7), Meghalaya (85.5), Dadra & Nagar Haveli (78.99), Arunachal Pradesh (63.66)
20-35%	Manipur (34.4), Tripura (30.95), Madhya Pradesh (23.27), Sikkim (22.36), Orissa (22.21)
10-12%	Assam (12.8), Rajasthan (12.4), Daman and Diu (11.54)
5-10%	Andaman & Nicobar (9.54), Maharashtra (9.27), Bihar (7.66), Andhra Pradesh (6.3), West Bengal (5.6)
1-5%	Karnataka (4.26), Himachal Pradesh (4.2), Kerala (1.1), Tamil Nadu (1.03)
Les than 1%	Uttar Pradesh (0.21), Goa (0.03)
None	Chandigarh, Delhi, Haryana, Pondicherry, Punjab

proportion is independent of the size. There are six states and Union territories that have more than 60 per cent tribals; five others have tribal population of between 20 and 35 per cent; another three have 10 to 12 per cent; five are in the category of 5 to 10 per cent; four in the category of 1 to 5 per cent; and two states have less than one per cent. There is none in the range of 35 to 60 per cent. See the distribution in Table 2.

The 2001 Census puts the scheduled tribe population at 84.3 million, constituting 8.2 per cent of the total population of India. However, the regionwise distribution in percentage terms remains the same.

There is a wide diversity in terms of the literacy rates in these tribal groups. In 1991, the overall literacy rate for the scheduled tribes was 29.6 per cent, as compared to 16.33 per cent in 1981.

A Naga warrior

But the rate of literacy varies from 82.73 per cent in Mizoram and 80.58 per cent in Lakshadweep to 17.16 per cent in Andhra Pradesh. Those having more than 50 per cent literacy include, in addition to Mizoram and Lakshadweep, Nagaland (60.59), Manipur (53.63), Sikkim (59.01), Kerala (57.22), and Meghalaya (56.62). Literacy among the tribal population in Andaman & Nicobar, Tamil Nadu, and Bihar was around 27 per cent, and in Orissa, West Bengal, and Madhya Pradesh, around 22 per cent. Tribes in Rajasthan had 19.44 per cent literacy. What is significant is the point that while the literacy rate has risen in the decade, 1981-91, the actual number of illiterates has increased by 58 per cent. Thus, eradication of illiteracy and universalization of primary education are the major challenges for tribal development in India.

Racial and Linguistic Distribution

As was said in the first chapter, India is a multi-racial and multilingual country. This is also reflected in India's tribal population. The prehistory and ancient history of this country is replete with instances of interaction between the natives and outsiders arriving in the country with their distinctive racial features, languages, and cultures. The older residents either surrendered themselves to the victor group or planned escapes to retire in the mountainous regions. The topography provided them natural protection and helped them lead a secluded existence, preserving their culture. Those who developed equations with the arriving outsiders, however, continued to stay and their interactions led to intermarriages and sharing of cultural practices, including religion, language, food habits, and dressing patterns. That is why the racial types found in India contain many primitive strains and represent elements from all the main races of mankind. According to B.S. Guha, who proposed a racial classification of India at the time of the 1931 Census, tribal India is represented by the

Negritos, the Proto-Australoids, and the Mongoloids (the Palaeo-Mongoloids and the Tibeto-Mongoloids). Guha was of the view that the Negritos were the 'first comers' to the country and are the real 'autochthones'. The distinguishing mark of this race was the shape and form of the hair, which is separated into locks by being twisted either side into spirals. They were also pygmy in stature (below 5 feet), with small heads, bulbous foreheads, smooth brow ridges, and feeble chins. Their arms were longer than their legs and had deep pigmentation. The Andamanese, the Kadars, Palayans, and Irulas are linked to this racial type.

The Proto-Australoid type is found among the majority of tribes in peninsular India. They are also dark like the Negritos, but their hair is not frizzly or woolly. Their brow ridges are better developed, but their noses have sunken roots. The word, *nishad*, in Sanskrit literature was probably used for this group of people – noseless with darker skin and a peculiar speech. The tribes that correspond to this racial type are the Chenchu, Kurumba, Yeruva, Ho, Munda, Gond, Khond, Santal, Oraon, and the Birhor.

The Mongoloid type is to be found amongst the tribes of the sub-Himalayan region and Eastern India. The Mongoloids have very scanty hair on their face and body. They possess prominent cheek bones and have arrested development of the nasal skeleton. The most distinguishing mark is the epicanthic fold of the eye, though it is not so marked amongst the Palaeo-Mongoloids.

Language also helps in classifying people. But since language is a learned behaviour, unlike race, which is genetically inherited, it is not coterminous with race. People of the same race can speak different languages. And people speaking the same language can belong to different races. In India, the situation is further complicated by the fact that most people speak more than one language. The languages spoken in India belong to four distinct types as under:

1. The Indo-European, particularly its Indo-Aryan branch;
2. The Dravidian;

3. The Austro-Asiatic: the Munda and Kol branches, and
4. The Sino-Tibetan: the Tibeto-Burman branch.

Among the Indian tribes, there is a preponderance of the last three types. Languages belonging to the Dravidian family are spoken by the Gonds of Madhya Pradesh, Khonds of Orissa (who speak Kui), Malto in Rajmahal Hills, and the Toda in the Nilgiri Hills. These languages are 'agglutinative' in structure. The Santal, Munda, Ho, Kharia, Bhumij, Korku, Khasi, Gadaba, Savra, and the Nicobarese speak Austro-Asiatic languages. The tribes in the Himalayan region and Eastern India speak Sino-Tibetan languages. Due to contact with the languages of the rest of the country, and particularly with English, many tribal languages have lost their purity. Their phonetic systems have been affected and their vocabulary has been greatly enlarged with the incorporation of many alien words. Many tribal languages are on the verge of extinction. Some of the states of the Northeast have adopted English as their official language. In some cases, modern, educated tribals have attempted to revive their languages by using them with the Roman script.

There are 23 tribal languages that are each spoken by more than 100,000 (one lakh) people. These are Santhali, Gondi, Bhili, Oraon (or Kurukh), Lambadi, Ho, Mundari, Vagdi, Meithei (or Mainpuri), Banjari (or Labhani), Kondh, Bhilali, Savra, Garo, Khasi, Kui, Korku, Bara Bodo, Lushei, Paraja, Maria, Koya, and Mikir.[3] Santhali has the largest number of speakers, followed by Mikir. Other languages fall between these extremes. However, it must be kept in mind that this statistic is in terms of mother tongue collected at the time of the 1951 Census. Many tribals speak more than one language and at times have better linguistic competence in languages other than the mother tongue; this is more so in the case of educated tribals and also those who are frequently in contact with their non-tribal neighbours. Tribal political leaders from Jharkhand and Chhatisgarh, for example, speak fluent Hindi.

Levels of Economy

The tribes of India can also be classified on the basis of their traditional economic organization, material culture, and levels of technology. However, the tribal groups in India cannot be put into rigidly defined categories because the forces of regional and national economy have influenced all of them. The self-sufficiency of their economies has been broken considerably. Prior to their exposure and interaction with the non-tribals, the tribes in India could be classified into four categories:

1. *Tribes Depending on the Forests:* These tribes are food gatherers. They include the Kadars of Kochi, Malapantaram of Travancore, Pulliyan of Tamil Nadu, and the Paniyan of Wynaad;
2. *Tribes with an Economy Midway between Food Gathering and Primitive Agriculture:* For example, the Kamar and the Baiga of Madhya Pradesh, and the Reddi of the Bison Hills;
3. *Tribes Depending upon Some Form of Agriculture with Forest Products as a Secondary Support:* The bulk of the tribal population, particularly in Northeastern, and Central India, belong to this category; and
4. *A New Economic Category of Industrial Workers or Labourers in Tea Gardens:* Following the growth of industry in India, particularly in the tribal belts, the tribals of Bihar, Bengal, and Assam have become labourers and even migrated to plantations.

If the tribal population is plotted on the physical map of India, one would easily see the correspondence between geographical location and economic organization. In the Northeast, terrace cultivation of a more or less settled type is the dominant economic activity. In Central India, there is a preponderance of swidden, popularly known as shifting cultivation, or slash and burn cultivation. Amongst the tribes of Southern India, food gathering and some form of shifting cultivation is more common. There are also some nomadic groups who are snake charmers and acrobats; some of them also indulge in criminal activities.

Hunters and Food Gatherers

These tribals have a low level of technology, which reduces their capacity to exploit natural resources. Their major preoccupation is to collect daily and seasonal food supplies, as they do not know how to preserve them for consumption later. For example, the Onge of the Andaman Islands engage in pig hunting during the rainy season – May to September. While small teams of men go out hunting, women and children collect firewood, roots, tubers, and berries. They also make baskets, mats, and nets. During the cool season – September to March – they collect the larvae of cicadas and beetles, fruits, and also go out fishing and turtle hunting. Honey is collected during the summer months.

The Cholanaickan of Kerala survive on various edible roots and berries. They collect ginger, turmeric, cardamom, and sweet potato, which are bartered for tobacco, rice, and dried fish. They also engage in fishing. For fishing, they use three different techniques, namely poisoning the fish with the bark of the *enga* tree, using rod and string, or draining out the water from a part of the river or stream. They also trap monkeys, rabbits, and other small animals.

The Kharia of Purulia are now hardpressed with the disappearance of the forests. They have taken up jobs as agricultural labourers. They also make brooms, fish traps, and bidis (country cigarettes made by wrapping tobacco in tendu leaves). They eat rats, birds, and hare. They also eat the meat of dead cattle.

Pastoral Groups

The pastoral tribes are found in the entire cis-Himalayan region. The Gujjars of the Kashmir valley, known as the dairymen, move from place to place in search of grazing pastures, going up to the heights during the summers and returning to the plains during the winters. The Gaddis of the Chamba and Kangra valleys in Himachal Pradesh are also pastorals tending sheep, but they also specialize in spinning, weaving, and as blacksmiths. According to one description, the Gaddis are a predominantly agricultural people with a subsidiary interest in sheep grazing. W.H. Newell describes them as 'entirely Hindu' and says that "many of their *purohits* can recite large passages from the *Ramayana* by heart. They live in small villages scattered along the banks of the Upper Ravi and Budl Nadl rivers in Chamba State and along the foothills of the Dhaula Dhar range... During the winter, they care for their sheep in the Kangra valley; in the spring, they cross over the range to Bharmaur and to the Tibetan-speaking district of Lahul; in the autumn, they climb up to the high 12,000 feet pastures on the intervening range, gradually being forced down to the Kangra plain again for the winter. But in spite of the fact that they are so largely a pastoral people, by no means does every house in the village keep sheep, but every single shepherd on the mountain has a fixed home... During the winter, large numbers of Gaddis, who have no sheep, move from the central district either to stay with relatives on the Kangra side or else to look for odd jobs on the Punjab plains." Shepherds from Northern Rajasthan also make similar journeys crossing Haryana, Delhi, and Punjab to the higher altitudes in Himachal Pradesh in the summers and returning with their herd during the winters. On their way, they shear the wool from the sheep and sell it for a living.

In the South, the Todas of the Nilgiri Hills provide a good example of pastoral living. Besides being dairymen, they are also known as a polyandrous people – the women have more than one husband.

Shifting Cultivators or Swiddeners[4]

It is estimated that nearly three million tribals in India subsist on one form or the other of swidden. In local dialects, this kind of practice is generally referred to as *jhuming*, particularly in the Northeast. It is also called *bewar* (in Madhya Pradesh), *kurwa* (in Santal Pargana), and *podu* (in Orissa and Andhra Pradesh). The main feature of this kind of cultivation is that fields are cleared of their vegetation by felling the trees and burning them, and then crops are grown on the ashes. After harvesting the crop, the field is abandoned for some years for the vegetation to grow once again, and the swiddeners move to another field. Of course, differences exist with regard to the kind of trees that are felled and the length of the fallow period. Swidden cultivation is classified in several ways. There are five typologies in vogue: (1) based on the relationship between cultivation and the fallow period (short cultivation-short fallow, short cultivation-long fallow, long cultivation-long fallow or abandonment, and permanent field tree crops associated with the use of swiddening for rice); (2) historical background of the swiddeners (pioneers, established swiddeners, and incipient swiddeners); (3) degree of dependence on swiddening (exclusive dependence, major dependence, contingent dependence, marginal dependence); (4) phases of land cultivation (simple shifting cultivation, recurrent cultivation, recurrent cultivation with continuously cultivated plots, and continuous cultivation; and (5) mixed typology (combining vegetation systems, migration patterns, rotation system, clearance techniques, cropping pattern, and tools employed).

Forms of Social Organization

While there are broad similarities in the social organization of the various tribal groups, the differences are also quite significant. Stratification along age, sex, locality, clan, and phratry is common to all. Totemism in some form exists amongst all. Belief in the supernatural and in the power of magic is also a recurrent theme. The clan organization provides rules for exogamy. While the tribe is spread in a number of villages, it constitutes one community in the sense that it remains an endogamous group. Where a tribal group becomes part of the wider rural society, it assumes the character of a caste. Like the tribe, a caste is also endogamous, but what distinguishes it from the tribe is the fact that the caste is a unit of a system composed of different endogamous groups. The tribal social organization does not generally have endogamous units as subgroups, but the group as a whole is an in-marrying entity.

Many of the tribal communities in India have dormitories to train their youth in matters of sexual union, cooperative endeavour, and community life. These dormitories may be separate for the two sexes or common. The Muria Gonds of Madhya Pradesh call these dormitories *ghotuls* and they are common for boys and girls. Young, unmarried boys and girls gather here together in the evenings for dance and entertainment and to sleep. The ghotuls are of two types, jodidar and mundi-badalana. The first type of ghotuls are meant for permanent pairs, whereas in the second type, boys and girls are required to change their partners after a specified period. Among the Bhotias of the Himalayan hills, the dormitory is called *rang bang* and young girls entertain their boyfriends with drinks and beds. The Naga dormitory, called *morung*, is only for boys. The Memis have the *ikhnichi* for boys and the *iloichi* for girls. The Garo dormitory is called the *nok-pant*. The Oraons have the *dhumkuria;* the Jen Kurumba, the *pundale mane;* the Bondo, the *Selani dingo*; the Ho and the Munda, the *gitiora*.

Tribal India has both patriarchal and matriarchal family structures. The matriarchal societies are the Khasi and the Garo of Northeastern India, and the Kadar, Irula, and the Palayan of the South. Among the Khasis, it is the daughters who run the family, and the husband is only a *yu shang kha,* – meaning 'producer of children', – having no rights over the property of the wife's family. In the Sitong tribe, a husband cannot visit his wife during the day. Amongst the Garo, the sons-in-law come to reside with the family of their wives and separate living arrangements are made for them. However, the youngest daughter (called *nokna dona)* continues to live with her mother. If the mother is widowed, she is allowed to marry her son-in-law, the husband *(nokrom)* of the nokna dona. Thus, the mother and the daughter share the same husband. Of course, this is done to retain the inheritance right with the youngest daughter; the widowed mother may not have sexual congress with her son-in-law, though he is her husband legally.

Among the patrilineal tribes, there is prevalence of polygyny, men having more than one wife. But there are also groups, like the Todas of the Nilgiri Hills and the Khasa of Jaunsar-Bawar (who are not accorded tribal status), who practise polyandry (women having more than one wife); among the Khasa, these husbands are brothers (like the Pandavas), but among the Todas, they may not be related at all. Where husbands are brothers, it is called fraternal polyandry.

Needless to say that with the spread of education and contact with the outside world, many of these practices have been given up.

Degrees of Cultural Contact: A Typology

As we have mentioned above, the tribes are no longer secluded. Their contact with the neighbouring villages and towns have increased continuously. Christian missionaries have a long history of working among tribals, with the result that many of them have been converted to Christianity. Several efforts have been made in the past to classify the tribes in terms of their culture contact. Building upon them, Yogesh Atal proposed the following classification in 1963:[5]

I. Tribal Communities Living in their Original Habitat
   a. Relatively Isolated: Retaining most of the characteristics of their social organization and culture, despite some culture contact (the Kadars);
   b. Two or More Tribal Groups Living in the Same Area: Such groups maintain mutual contact, and yet remain isolated from other non-tribal groups (the Todas, Kotas, and Badagas);
   c. Living with Other Tribal/Religious Groups in the Same Community: These have the following subtypes:
      (i) Followers of their own religion, retaining most of the characteristics of their social organization and culture;
      (ii) While remaining separate from other religious groups, accept the leadership and domination of the other groups;
      (iii) Those moving towards Hinduization;
      (iv) Hinduized
         1. Tribes that have been forced to accept the degraded status of untouchables;
         2. Those enjoying high status, and
         3. Those assigned status in the middle ranges of the Hindu hierarchy, and
      (v) Baptised in other religions than Hindu
         1. Towards conversion, and
         2. Converts

II. Tribal Groups Living Away from Their Original Habitat
   a. Settled in Neighbouring Villages: These could also be classified into five categories as in I (c);
   b. Living in separate villages in other areas, such as Bhoksa of Nainital; and
   c. Settled in industrial centres or cities, or in tea plantations, military recruits, and others.

Development Planning for the Tribal Areas

The tribal areas are relatively backward. Their relative isolation obstructed the winds of change; even culture contacts with the outside world brought in many problems. It was surmised that the changes occurring among the tribals were associated with the fact of culture contact. Contact with outside settlers is an age-old phenomenon. Through such contacts, the tribes got involved in a sort of tribe-caste continuum to the extent that those tribes that freely interacted and even shared the same habitat were treated as castes. Processes of Hinduization and *Sanskritization* changed their socio-religious profiles. Many of the tribal deities got enshrined in the 'temple of Hinduism' and many elements of the Hindu Great Tradition got parochialized in the tribal settings. With the advent of British colonial rule, the tribals came in contact with Christianity and adopted several elements of Westernization, including modern forms of government and a legal system that challenged customary law. In the post-independence phase, the programmes of planned development and externally induced cultural change have affected the ways of life of these people.

The phenomenon of cultural contact is held responsible for a variety of problems faced by the tribals. The problems relate to (i) the exploitation of the tribals by outside contractors, money-lenders, and politicians; (ii) the problem of land alienation and bonded labour; (iii) health related problems, including venereal diseases; (iv) the effort of Christian missionaries during British rule to convert the tribals to Christianity and, consequently, to discard many of their traditions; (v) depopulation; (vi) the British policy of divide and rule, resulting in the creation of identity crisis and hurting the national solidarity being forged by the freedom fighters; and (vii) adverse effects on tribal customary law, particularly with regard to land rights and transfer of land.

Initially disturbed by the vanishing tribal cultures and the fact that tribal societies were being afflicted by the ill-effects of culture contact, such as spread of venereal diseases, skin ailments, serfdom, and even prostitution, many advocated preservation of the tribal cultures. As a consequence, some anthropologists were charged with 'keeping the tribals in a zoo'. Verrier Elwin, who strongly argued the tribal case, contested the allegation, but maintained that tribal rights must be respected.

As against this, some Indian scholars, particularly social reformer Thakkar Bapa and sociologist G.S. Ghurye, advocated a policy of assimilation into mainstream Hindu society.

Both these arguments were regarded as extremist viewpoints. Neither was it possible to keep the tribals in constant isolation, nor to merge their identities through assimilation.

In the ensuing debate in the 1950s, it was made clear that there was a need to properly plan the programmes of culture change. The problems of the tribal people should first be carefully and scientifically studied and then appropriate strategies evolved to solve them. An ad hoc and overly enthusiastic approach of philanthropy could be more damaging to the cause of the tribals. What anthropologists such as S.C. Dube have suggested in this regard has been summarized below:

1. Systematic studies of the social organization and values of the tribal communities should be undertaken.
2. The problems of the tribal groups differ relative to their technological, economic, and cultural development, and the solutions will also differ accordingly.
3. We must understand the factors and forces of tribal unity.
4. We must analyse tribal cultures in terms of change-prone and change-resistant aspects.
5. The tribe should be viewed in a holistic perspective in which all the parts of its culture are seen as related to one another. Change brought about in any part is likely to have repercussions in other parts.

6. Administrators and social workers working in the tribal areas must be properly trained in tribal cultures and should have an anthropological perspective.
7. Development projects for the tribal areas should establish a proper match between tribal needs and national goals.
8. There should be continued monitoring and evaluation of projects so that corrective actions can be taken against unanticipated harmful effects.

Since independence, a number of projects were initiated to develop the tribal areas. Reviewing the progress, the Study Team on Tribal Development Programmes, headed by Shilu Ao, found in 1969 that the development of these areas was uneven. Ao recommended more concentrated action in those areas where the tribals were still leading a primitive existence. The Fifth Five-Year Plan (1974-79) prepared a Tribal Sub-Plan (TSP), addressing the needs of the extremely backward tribal communities with complete funding from the Central government. A special workshop was convened in 1975 to evolve the criteria for the identification of such backward groups. Three criteria were proposed: (1) pre-agricultural level of technology; (2) low level of literacy; and (3) stagnant or declining population.

Following these criteria, 74 tribal groups in 15 states and Union territories were identified as 'primitive'. For these primitive tribal groups, a new Central Sector Scheme has been introduced from 1998-99, under which financial assistance is given to Integrated Tribal Development Projects (ITDP), Tribal Research Institutes (TRIs), and non-governmental organizations (NGOs). A sum of Rs 10.71 crore was sanctioned for this scheme in 2000-01. There are 194 ITDPs in the country in those blocks where the scheduled tribe population is more than 50 per cent of the total population. In addition, the TSP under the Modified Area Development Approach (MADA), covers places where there are at least

5,000 tribals. There are 252 such MADA pockets. Special Central assistance is also given to the states/UTs to supplement their efforts in tribal development. This assistance is given for income-generating schemes in the sectors of agriculture, horticulture, minor irrigation, animal husbandry, soil conservation, education, cooperatives, and small-scale cottage industries. In 2000-01, Rs 400 crore were given to the states for this purpose. Additional grants were also given for setting up residential schools and ashram schools.

In 2001, the government of India set up a National Scheduled Tribes Financial Development Corporation. This is an apex institution for financing economically viable projects for scheduled tribes. There is also a Central Sector Scheme of Grain Banks in tribal villages, which was launched in 1996-97. The main aim of this scheme is to provide safeguards against fall in the nutritional standards of scheduled tribes living in remote rural areas.

Tribal India, like the rest of the country, is in the throes of change. The large number of tribes in our Northeast have a high degree of literacy and numerical predominance in many of the states in which they reside. They are also politically active. Change has affected almost all the tribes so much that the old monographs written about them read like unbelievable tales.

There is need to revisit many of the tribal groups and study them to find out how much change has occurred in them and what institutions of their primitive past still continue to guide their lives. Their diversity not withstanding, they are a part of the unity of India.

Notes

1. For example, the Bhils living in a mixed village in the Mewar area of Rajasthan are called *gameti* – literally, the village dwellers. They are treated as a separate caste and are served by a Brahman priest on occasions such as marriage. The difference was that while the other groups used ghee as the cooking medium in a feast, the Bhils used sesame oil. But this distinction must be fading as oil is now universally used for frying *pooris* by all, even in the cities.
2. S.C. Dube (ed.), *Antiquity to Modernity in Tribal India,* Vol. I, 1998, Inter-India Publications, New Delhi, pp. 4-5.
3. They are listed in descending order in terms of number of speakers.
4. Swidden is an old English dialect word meaning 'a burned clearing'. This term was resurrected in 1955 by E. Ekwall to describe 'shifting' or slash-and-burn cultivation because this refers to the type of agricultural technology. For detail, see Yogesh Atal (ed.), *Swidden Cultivation in Asia* (3 Volumes), 1983, UNESCO, Bangkok.
5. Yogesh Atal, 'The Tribe-Caste Question', 1963, in *Bulletin of the Bihar Tribal Research Institute*, Ranchi, Vol.V, No. 1, pp. 21-22.

6

Varna and *Jati*

In this chapter . . .

For centuries, visitors to India were struck by its distinctive social order, which divided people into rigid occupation based groups. The membership of these groups was defined by birth and it remained unchanged. Deriving from the Portuguese word *casta,*[1] these groups are known as castes in English. In Indian vernacular, the word used for them is *Jati*. These *jatis* are said to belong to one of four *varnas*. The entire system of *varna* and *jati* is called the caste system.

Although *jati* or caste is generally associated with the Hindu social system, this feature characterizes Indian society as a whole. That is why one finds the terms *Adijati* and *Vanyajati* used for the 'tribe', which has no equivalent in Hindi or Sanskrit; in fact, common men refer to the tribes as *jatis*, with the result that many tend to think that they belong to the Hindu fold.

Caste is considered a unit for the local social system and is used as a generic term for all in-marrying groups inhabiting the area, including tribals and other religious groups. The caste system has been described as something peculiar and unique to India and specific to Hindus. Many sociologists and anthropologists have contrasted India's caste society with the class society of the West.

In sociology textbooks, the two concepts – that of caste and class – are negatively defined: "Caste is a closed class; and Class is an open caste." In this sense, both are structural categories. Those who regard caste as a 'structural' feature have argued that the caste system is found in non-Hindu contexts as well. Examples are given of the *Paikchong* of Korea and the *Ita* of Japan, who have a status similar to the Shudras. On this basis, it is suggested that Korean and Japanese societies exhibit rudimentary forms of the caste system. Similarly, those who studied the Deep South of the US have talked about the white-black relationship in caste terms. In India as well, we find that despite conversion to Islam or Christianity, the converts have carried their castes to their new affiliation and thus stratified these religions along caste lines. It is also important to note that in both these religions, there are several sects which practise endogamy and thus behave like castes. This is also true of Sikhism, Jainism, and Buddhism, which rose as protest movements against the Brahmanical caste system, but remain divided along caste lines.

Making caste synonymous with the Indian social system renders caste as a 'cultural' category, but contrasting it with class makes it a 'structural' category. This is a significant difference. When used as a cultural category, caste becomes a unique culture-specific feature. Treating caste as an exclusively Indian phenomenon, a reference is made to the Hindu lawgiver, Manu, who is regarded as its architect. Such scholars focus on finding out the cultural – religious and philosophical – justifications provided by society for its origin and continuance. Inequalities amongst the castes have generally been seen in terms of ritual purity and pollution and the practice of untouchability. The evil aspects of the system – such as oppression and untouchability – are highlighted and a reformist stand is taken to remove the evils of the system.

As a structural category, the way most sociologists employ the term, it is a group consisting of networks of actual or potential affinal (related through marriage) and consanguineous or cognate (related through blood or birth) kinship ties. In small village communities, a caste is generally represented by cognate kins and, thus, it is only a fraction of the caste. Moreover, in Northern India, such a group is generally exogamous as, unlike the South, no parallel or cross-cousin marriages or marriages between the mother's brother (*mama)* and sister's daughter (*bhanji*) are permitted. Thus, when we talk of a caste in a village, we talk only of a kin group belonging to a particular caste that has a regional spread. To understand the full functioning of the caste system, one has to go beyond the confines of a village. Within a village, castes are usually represented by a group of interconnected families – a lineage or a *gotra* – but relations between castes can be observed in day-to-day interactions. Thus, caste is regarded as a horizontal unity cutting across several villages, while the village is a vertical unity of castes. But what one observes in the microcosm of a village cannot be generalized over cities and towns, even within the same region. The size of the locality significantly influences the functioning of the caste.

Caste is a much misunderstood term. It is employed for different kinds of groupings both by writers as well as common people. It has been, and is being, used for *varna* (no English equivalent is satisfactory, some literally translate it as colour, signifying race; others call it a caste cluster, still others use it for caste and use the term sub-castes for *jatis*). People also use the word caste

A Dharnarajapuram Brahman and his wife (Photo 1974, by Pauline Kolenda)

for *gotra,* and even for a family title, or for a regional group. Sociologically, these are all wrong usages. For example, Brahman is not a *jati*, it is a *varna*, just as Kshatriya, Vaishya and Shudra are *varnas* in the Hindu system of Chaturvarnya (four-*varna* division). Similarly, a *gotra* (such as Bharadwaj, Vashishtha), or a family title (such as Kothari, Bhandari, Grover, Malik) is different from a caste. A caste consists of several families belonging to different *gotras,* or family titles. There are also *avataks* and *pravars*, which distinguish different lineages and clans from each other.

Another term used for caste is *biradari.* In common parlance, people talk of *jat-biradari*. The term *biradar* is taken from Persian,

An untouchable sweeper woman (Photo 1955, by J. Michael Mahar)

meaning 'brother', and thus signifies brotherhood. Since both jat and biradari are used with a hyphen in between, many regard this as a synonym of caste; others feel that it is a term for the kin group. In the latter sense, the term *biradari* becomes a subgroup within a caste. Technically, they are called *exogamous* (marrying outside or not allowing marriage within). All such groupings within a caste are out-marrying units; using this word for the group residing in a village is thus justified, but is mistaken as a synonym of caste. In this context, it is important to note that when the Muslims use the term *biradari,* they do not imply its exogamous character, because Islam allows parallel-cousin marriages, i.e., marriage between children of two brothers or two sisters, which is regarded as incest amongst the Hindus. As an exception, one may quote the Meos of Alwar district in Rajasthan, who have converted to Islam; they do not permit parallel cousin marriages though their adopted religion allows such unions. The Meos are treated in the local social system as a caste, though of a different religion.

The key characteristic of caste is endogamy (in-marrying, or allowing its members to marry within the group). Thus, people of the same caste marry within that group, but outside exogamous groups such as family, lineage, clan or *gotra*, or *biradari*.[2] Of course, there are groups that not only allow marriages within the caste, but also in other castes. This practice is called either hypergamy (*anulom*) or hypogamy (*pratilom*).[3] In both circumstances, caste remains endogamous. But when no such marriages are allowed outside of the caste, the group is technically called isogamous.[4]

Thus, it is wrong to term Sindhis, Bengalis, Punjabis, and Tamilians as castes. These appellations describe the region from which a person hails, or a linguistic group, not his caste. In the regions of Sindh, Bengal, Punjab, and Tamil Nadu not everybody belongs to the same caste. Each region is divided into a number of castes, and each of these castes is divided into a number of exogamous groups (*gotras* or lineages).

Similarly, every *jati* is not a subcaste. The word subcaste must be reserved for the group that has separated from a known caste in the not very distant past and has some common elements. Thus, several castes of the Brahman *varna* are not subcastes of the Brahman. A subcaste is generally created as a result of fission of a bigger group.

A Hindu, thus, belongs to his family; that family is part of a lineage, of a *laukik gotra* (a localized clan), a *rishi gotra* (an eponymous clan), a *jati*, and a *varna*. In the south, a *varna* (particularly the Brahman) is divided into sub-*varnas*, each of which has a number of castes belonging to it.[5] An individual can use any of these as his last name. Thus, the last name does not always signify

An artisan: Kumhar (Potter)

caste. For example, people belonging to the Brahman *varna*, but to different castes, can use Sharma as the last name, but that would not signify their caste. Moreover, this suffix is also used by people belonging to the carpenter caste (*suthar*), and also by barbers (*nai*), both of whom do not belong to the Brahman *varna*. So is the case with the suffix Verma, which is used both by the people of the Kshatriya *varna* and some of the Kayasthas.[6]

What is important to remember is that in our day-to-day dealings, we tend to blur these distinctions with the result that we tend to associate many things with caste. The fact of the matter is that not many people understand these differences and the growing indifference towards understanding the subtleties of the caste system is an indication of how greatly we have departed from the original formulation. Caste thus figures in our conversations and in our behaviour patterns, but its perception does not match either with Manu, whose *Smriti* is often decried, or with the objective sociological definition. Today's caste cannot be reduced to Manu's formulation. As it has evolved over the centuries, caste has widely distanced itself from the ideological prescription of Manu. Anthropological and sociological studies of caste carried out in the country in the last five or six decades have helped to negate the 'book view' and the 'upper caste view' of caste. Here we will talk of caste in contemporary India.

To summarize, there are five main difficulties in defining caste:[7]

1. *Difficulties Arising from a Variety of Social Organizations:* It is important to remember that all castes were not built on the same model. The system has grown slowly and gradually through fusion and fission of existing groups and incorporation of other groups. Different castes had different origins. There is a wide variety of practices in different regions and different castes within the same region. This makes it difficult to formulate a satisfactory definition of caste;
2. *Difficulties Emerging from Ignorance about or Indifference Towards Other Castes by the Local People:* In the caste context, people are grouped in different ways. Caste is used, depending upon the situation, for a *varna*, subcaste, religious group, or even a regional group. It is also used for exogamous groups within a caste;
3. *Difficulties Emerging from the Confusion between the Ideal and the Real:* The ideal of the four *varnas* is no longer clearly applicable in today's context, because all the castes of today cannot be said to be the descendants of the original four *varnas*. The location of the new entrants in the four-fold Hindu hierarchy has not been easy. The Census enumerators of 1891 found as many as 2,300,000 castes in the country and found it hard to

determine their eligibility and location in the *varna* scheme;

4. *Difficulties Emerging from the Fluidity in the Caste System:* Contrary to the prevalent notion that the caste system is rigid, students of Indian society have discovered many processes in operation that have changed caste boundaries, for example, instances of analogous castes getting amalgamated. There are also cases of a caste having got split into two or more groups, first as factions and later as independent castes, cutting all ties with the parent body. At times, people who have been ostracized for breaking the rule of endogamy have created separate castes.
5. *Difficulties Emerging from a Common Nomenclature:* There are castes, which are better known by the name of the occupation pursued by their members, or the locality from which they migrated, or the language they speak. There is also a widespread effort by castes and certain individuals within the group to adopt a new name or use a surname associated with other groups. This also creates confusion. In addition, there are some names that are found in different regions, but the groups bearing the same name have functioned as separate endogamous groups, and thus as separate castes, despite the common name. Yadav, Nai, Lohar, etc., are examples of this. In the present day context, use of the word Dalit (which has replaced the word Harijan given by Gandhi) is for a whole cluster of castes that are recognized by the constitution as scheduled castes, as also for the backward classes and scheduled tribes. The many groups included in this category are, sociologically speaking, different castes in terms of their endogamous character. Like *varna*, such groups are caste clusters of identical rank, but not a single caste. It should also be emphasized that hierarchy exists even within a given *varna* – all Brahman castes,

> for example, are not of the same rank. Similarly, all the scheduled castes are not untouchables, and the castes covered under this category also observe ritual distances from each other and prefer to practise endogamy.

Definitions of caste are many. Some have defined caste as a *unit*; others have talked of the caste system. There are others who have combined the traits of the unit and the system without making a clear-cut distinction. By using the term both for caste (that is *jati*) and *varna*, as also for caste and subcaste, a good deal of confusion has been created. There is no vernacular word for the subcaste.

The *varna* system of the Vedic times did distinguish between priests (Brahmans), nobles and warriors (Kshatriyas or Rajanyas), tillers of the soil (Vaishyas), and menial workers and slaves (Shudras). These functions were regarded as hereditary, "exceptions were freely allowed...The Brahmans had... the possibilities of a warrior. The *rsis* of old were agriculturists and sometimes warriors, too."[8] Ghurye also said that though "the classes had come to be stereotyped by the end of the Vedic period, it was not altogether impossible for an upward and downward change to occur".[9] Instances are available of Kshatriya kings becoming Brahmans by giving up some practices and adopting others. The *Harivansha Puran* says that two sons of Vaishya Nabhgarishta became Brahmans. Even Shudras could change their status. The Pokhar Sevak Brahmans of Rajasthan trace their ancestry to a Mer. The Vyasokta Brahmans of Bengal are said to be the descendants of a Shudra. Many who are called Rajputs and thus acknowledged to be Kshatriyas are said to be late arrivals as 'tribal groups'; similarly, the Gujjars and Jats also came from abroad and got assimilated into the caste system. The latter groups are also found among the Muslims, indicating conversion to that religion and yet carrying the baggage of caste.

The term subcaste should be used only for those groups that have split up and become endogamous groups in themselves, but still retain some links with the original unit. This split may occur either because a significant section moves to a distant place or adopts a different occupation. For example, the various gypsy castes of South-East Punjab and Uttar Pradesh have become endogamous units, though they were one group originally. The 1931 Census gives the example of the Khatik (butcher) caste, which got split into Bekanwala (pork butcher), Rajgar (mason), Sombatta (ropemaker), and Mewafarosh (fruiterer). Such subcastes continue to have marital linkages for some time, but finally stop intermarriages and become independent castes. A good example is of the Kaibarttas (in Uttar Pradesh, they are known as Kewat[10]) of Bengal. This group might have originally been a tribe. After coming into contact with other castes, this group divided itself occupationally into two groups. One group took over the calling of fishermen, and the other of farming. The fishermen dealt with *jal* (water) and were called Jaliya Kaibarttas, and the other group handled the *hal* (plough) and took the name of Haliya Kaibarttas. Since ploughing was rated higher, the Haliya Kaibarttas gave women in marriage to the Jaliyas, demanding a high bride price, but did not accept wives from them. Of course, this seems to be an exception because, generally, people of a higher caste take wives from the lower castes, but do not marry their daughters into a lower group (practice of hypergamy or *anulom*). In due course of time, the two Kaibartta subcastes became separate endogamous groups, and the Haliya Kaibarttas even changed their name to Mahishya.

There are also instances of fusion. At the time of the 1931 Census, there was a widespread movement among the various cattle-herding castes to use a common name, Yadav. These groups included the Ahirs, Ahars, Goalas, Gollas, Gops, and Idaiyans. Although these groups belonged to different cultural regions and used the same name, they did not become a single in-marrying group; thus, sociologically speaking, they remained separate castes. Yadav, thus, becomes a caste cluster or an equivalent of *varna*. They may be a political unity, but sociologically remain divided into separate castes in different regions.

A caste, that is *jati*, should be understood as a 'minimally' endogamous group. The prefix, minimally, is important. Below this level, the group is divided into exogamous groups. Without this qualification, caste would lose its sociological significance and cease to be a concept. All the groups above this level are equally endogamous. People marry within their own caste, within their own religion, within their own region, and within their own country. But the endogamy of the religion, region, or country is a feature that is universal. Hindus marry Hindus, but Hindu is not a caste. People of Mewar marry within Mewar, but Mewar is not a caste. Indians marry Indians, but India is not a caste.

There is another point that needs to be highlighted. A group's endogamous character should be understood in terms of the capability of the group to provide mates, that is to say that 'marriage within is prescribed and possible'. But this does not mean that marriages cannot take place outside. While discussing subcastes, we had said that in the initial phases of the split of the caste, the subgroups allowed marriages that could be hypergamous or hypogamous. Since hypergamy is practised 'in addition to' endogamy, the groups bear the caste character. Where endogamy is total, not allowing any hyper- or hypo-gamous unions, it should be called isogamy – a case of rigid endogamy.

Let us illustrate the practice of hypergamy or *anulom*. J.H. Hutton, in his *Caste in India* (Oxford University Press, 1961 edition), illustrates this practice among the Rarhi Brahmans of Bengal. To quote from Hutton:

> This caste is divided into subcastes known as Kulin and Srotriya, the latter being again subdivided into Siddha,

> Sadhya and Kashta Srotriyas. A man of the Kulin subcaste can take a wife from the Kulin, Siddha Srotriya or Sadhya Srotriya subcastes; a man from the Siddha Srotriya from his own or from the Sadhya Srotriya subcaste; a Sadhya Srotriya man or a Kashta Srotriya man can only take a wife from his own subcaste. Conversely, while a Kashta woman can marry only another Kashta Srotriya, a Sadhya can marry Sadhya, Siddha Srotriya, or Kulin, and a Siddha Srotriya woman can marry a man of her own sub-caste or a Kulin, while a Kulin woman can marry a Kulin only [1961: 53].

Among the Rajputs, hypergamous marriages have a different pattern. There, the various clans or *gotras* are ranked higher and lower and, generally, a bridegroom of superior status is sought for a girl. Thus, the boy marries into a clan of lower standing. It is the practice of hypergamy that led to the institution of dowry – putting a price on the bridegroom. Where hypogamy (*pratilom*) is practised, the bridegroom has to pay a bride price.

Thus, the 'basic attribute' of a caste unit is endogamy. The group has to be minimally endogamous. It may follow it rigidly and become (isogamous), or it may allow both marriages within and outside through hypergamy or hypogamy. Built into the concept of endogamy is the point that such endogamous groups are divided into exogamous groups, called clan or *gotra* or *got*. There are said to be eight Rishi *gotras* (also called *aarsh*) or eponymous clans. These are found in a number of castes across the two *varnas*, Brahman and Kshatriya. In addition to these are the *laukik* (meaning this worldly, or local) *gots*, which are in large numbers and they signify extended lineage groups. Generally, people are ignorant about the Rishi gotras and it is the laukik gotras, also called *avatank*, which are considered while fixing a marriage. In Northern India, for example, care is taken amongst the upper castes to avoid close relatives from both the father's side and mother's side by ensuring that the chosen mate does not belong to any of the *gotras* of closer kin of the parents.

The visibility of caste as a group is heightened when (a) all its members are recruited by birth alone (ascriptive recruitment) – that is, when the group becomes completely isogamous;[11] (b) the members pursue a common occupation; and (c) when the group has its own traditional council (Panchayat) to enforce caste norms over its members. (d) If the caste has a distinct name, not shared by any other group and (e) if its members can be identified by a distinctive dress pattern or naming pattern or certain practices, then it becomes easier to distinguish one caste from the other. It may be said that while endogamy is the *basic* attribute, the other attributes (b) and (c) mentioned above are 'sufficiently relevant' in the sense that their presence enhances the visibility of the group. Attributes (d) and (e) are 'peripheral' in that they definitely further enhance visibility, but their disappearance does not cause a major crisis in identity. When any of the sufficiently relevant attributes disappear, caste identification becomes somewhat difficult, but the continuity of the group is maintained through the practice of endogamy.

A caste is to be understood as a group within a society. It is recognized only in relation to other such groups in the society with which it interacts in the economic, political, social, and ritual spheres of life. This network outlines the working of the caste *system*. Thus, it is logical to define the caste system as a 'plurality of interacting endogamous groups (*jatis*) living a common culture'. Traditionally, these castes were arranged hierarchically as part of the *varna* system. And there existed a broad division of labour between them because of occupational specialization. The presence of all these three elements, in the context of ritual purity and pollution, made the caste system highly visible. Cultural definitions of purity and pollution, derived from the Hindu religion, made people to think that the Caste system was an exclusively Hindu phenomenon. In contemporary India, ritual dominance is gradually eroding yet caste persists. The concept of the caste system, with individual castes as units within it, helps us distinguish a caste from a tribe. A tribe may contain all the attributes of a caste unit, but it is not a part of a broader system consisting of similar such groups within the same territory. But when a tribe interacts with other castes, it becomes part of the caste system and is treated as a separate caste in interaction with other castes.

It must be emphasized that caste, as a structural category, is found in non-Hindu societies as well. "A clear-cut *varna* division," writes S.C. Dube, "is not found among the Christians and Muslims, but a distinction is made between high-caste and low-caste converts. The former identify themselves as Brahman Christians or Nayar Christians, or as Rajput or Tyagi Muslims". Writing about the situation of converted Christians, Dube says:

> The Indian Church now realizes that approximately 60 per cent of the 19 million Indian Christians are subjected to discriminatory practices and treated as second-class Christians or worse. In the South, Christians from the scheduled Caste are segregated both in their settlements and in the Church. Their *cheri* or colony is situated at some distance from the main settlement and is devoid of the civic amenities available to others. In church services, they are segregated to the right wing and are not allowed to read scriptural pieces during the service or to assist the priest. They are the last to receive the holy sacraments during baptism, confirmation, and marriage. The marriage and funeral processions of Christians from the low castes are not allowed to pass through the main streets of the settlement. Scheduled Castes converted to Christianity have separate cemeteries. The church bell does not toll for their dead, nor does the priest visit the home of the dead to pray. The dead body cannot be taken

into the church for the funeral service. Of course, there is no inter-marriage and little inter-dining among the 'high-caste' and the 'low-caste' Christians.[12]

Among the Muslims also, a distinction is made between the original and the convert Muslims. In common parlance, people talk of *sharif zat* (well-bred, or of higher caste) and *ajlaf zat* (common, or of lower caste). These distinctions govern decisions regarding marriage and inter-dining. The converts continue to practise their *jati*-linked occupations, which heighten the separate identity as in the caste system. Mention may be made of Muslim castes such as Julaha, Bhisti, Teli, and Kalal. It is significant that the Muslims are also divided into four divisions, namely Syed, Sheikh, Mughal, and Pathan. And these function as endogamous groups. In fact, among the Muslims, endogamy is much more restricted because both cross cousin and parallel cousin marriages are preferred.

It can be said that as an aspect of Indian social life, caste has crossed religious boundaries. Even within Hinduism, the practice of the system varies from region to region. The present-day system of caste cannot be understood in terms of the ideal prescribed in the sacred scriptures. With new entrants to the system and departures of some groups (through conversion) to other religions (Islam, Christianity, Jainism, Buddhism, Sikhism), the system has grown continually and become much more complex. Students of caste working in India's villages and towns have found it very difficult to construct a ritual hierarchy of the castes. All the castes do not neatly fall into the four *varnas* and the so-called 'fifth *varna*'. Occupationally, the castes have become much more differentiated. Moreover, there have been efforts on the part of the castes to move upwards in the ritual hierarchy. This process was noticed and elaborated by M.N. Srinivas in his essay on 'Sanskritization and Westernization', published in the *Far Eastern Quarterly* (Vol. XV, No. 4, 1956).

Caste and Change: *Sanskritization*

Srinivas has argued that "the caste system is far from a rigid system in which the position of each component caste is fixed for all time". Various pre-Aryan and non-Aryan people adopted the practices of the Vedic Aryans, which changed their outlook and ways of life. In fact, the growth in the number of castes is attributable to the continuous acceptance and assimilation of outsider groups into the Hindu fold. While these groups were accepted as Hindus, they retained the group identities determined by their birth. Acceptance also meant their location in the caste hierarchy. It is the change in the location of the caste hierarchy that characterizes the process of *Sanskritization*. Srinivas defined the concept of *Sanskritization* as: "...the process by which a 'low' caste or tribe or other group changes its customs, ritual, ideology, and style of life in the direction of a high, and frequently, 'twice-born' caste. Generally, such changes are followed by a claim to a higher position in the caste hierarchy than that traditionally conceded to the claimant caste by the local community. The claim is usually made over a period of time, in fact, a generation or two, before the 'arrival' is conceded."[13] *Sanskritization* usually presupposes either an improvement in the economic or political position of the group concerned, or a higher group self-consciousness resulting from its contact with a source of the Great Tradition of Hinduism, such as a pilgrim centre or monastery, or proselytizing sect.

The process of *Sanskritization* is a good example of reference group behaviour. The higher castes are treated by the lower castes as a reference group whom they emulate because of the prestige associated with it. On occasions, the upper castes may discourage such efforts to maintain their superiority and political and economic dominance. But field studies suggest that this process was widespread. Such upward mobility was always possible, particularly in the middle regions of the hierarchy. A low caste succeeded, in a generation or two, in climbing up by adopting vegetarianism and teetotalism and by *Sanskritizing* its ritual and pantheon. Tribal groups that were not part of Hinduism came to be treated as castes when they adopted Hindu practices and began interacting with other local castes. Since Hinduism is polytheistic, these groups continued worshipping their deities with some added rituals. Along with the new entrant groups, Hinduism went on absorbing local cultural beliefs. This is the reason that the local caste system represents a unique hierarchy of *jatis*. The same *jati* in two different cultural areas may occupy two different positions in the hierarchy. This is due to the differences in their *Sanskritization*, according to Srinivas.

Srinivas is of the view that the second *varna*, namely Kshatriya, has been the most open. It has accommodated all kinds of groups that had the effective possession of political power. "He who became chief or king had to become a Kshatriya, whatever his origins." A bard provided a genealogy linking the chief with a well-known Kshatriya lineage, or even to Sun or the Moon (*Suryavanshi* or *Chandravanshi*). The life style of the newly coronated king had to correspond to the Kshatriya way of life, duly supported by the Brahman priests. The Brahmans have always been predisposed to reverence power and they helped in legitimizing the authority of the chief. Various sects as well as pilgrim centres have also acted as agents of *Sanskritization*.

Srinivas has talked of two forms of caste mobility. One, 'in which a *jati* adopted, over a generation or two, the name and other attributes of a regionally prestigious dominant caste, which was not highly Sanskritized'; and two, 'in which a *jati* called itself a Brahman or Kshatriya or Vaishya (usually with a prefix), and this was accompanied by appropriate changes in its diet, style of life, and ritual'.

Analyzing social change in India, Srinivas noted the simultaneous operation of the twin processes of *Sanskritization* and Westernization, and found that the two were not always contradictory. In fact, in many cases, they reinforced each other. Because of these changes, it is not possible to understand today's caste in terms of the ideal of the *varna* system or the prescriptions of Manu.

Caste in Contemporary India

It is evident that caste in contemporary India cannot be understood via the scriptural texts. One is not sure at what stage the castes displayed a pattern of cumulative inequalities, but it is abundantly clear that today's castes represent dispersed inequalities. Those who might be regarded superior in the ritual sphere and in terms of purity and pollution, need not be necessarily superior in terms of political power or economic prowess. In the urbanized sections of society and amongst the educated, interactions are not guided by ritual considerations. Giving up of dress diacriticals has helped blur identities. Anthropologists pointed out in the 1960s that people employed a double standard: following traditional ways of interaction in the villages and ignoring such considerations in an urban milieu. When employing domestic servants, for example, little attention is given by the urban dweller to the caste of the candidate. In metropolitan centres, migrants from distant regions provide such domestic help and their claims as to their caste status cannot be easily verified. Also, people from the villages that have been engulfed by the process of suburbation have changed their traditional vocations and adopted new occupations, including domestic work, gardening, driving, etc.

Despite several departures from the ideal model derived from Manu, caste and the caste system has not disappeared in India. While the changes have been dramatic in matters of commensality and occupation, they have not mitigated caste distinctions. Today, inter-dining is a common feature, each caste is highly diversified occupationally, and untouchability is fast disappearing, particularly in the urban areas. It should be noted that not all occupations are caste-bound. While caste related occupations are still largely practised by a few members of the caste, and may not be taken up by people of other castes, several members belonging to the occupational caste engage themselves in open occupations that are not caste-bound. What has remained is the pursuit of certain caste-linked occupations by some section of that particular caste. It is delinking of caste from occupation that one can find even Brahmans selling shoes and leather goods, and some traditional leather working caste people engaged in teaching and administration. Thus, occupation is not a defining characteristic of castes any more. People abandon their traditional caste-related occupation and yet continue to belong to the caste in which they were born, and use that group for marriage. It is in this sense that Adrian Mayer calls caste the kindred of recognition.[14]

Even in the sphere of marriage, there are rising instances of intercaste marriages (labelled love marriages as against arranged marriages) and also of inter-regional intra-caste marriages.

It seems caste has changed its form. Traditional inter-caste relations based mainly on the principle of occupational specialization and the concepts of ritual purity and pollution are increasingly being disregarded. But caste is emerging as a political force. The horizontal unity of caste is being reinforced at levels higher than the minimally endogamous unit. Regarding castes as vote banks, numerical preponderance is being created by uniting people at the level of a caste cluster. It is in this frame that people use the referent of caste for such broader classes as Brahmans or Yadavs or Kshatriyas, or Jats, merging several castes belonging to these categories and hailing from different regions of the country. To understand the manner in which caste is assuming significance in the present-day polity, we will have to go beyond the village studies of the 1960s and the Indological treatises based on sacred texts.

Caste has not disappeared – it has merely shown its resilience to adapt to the changing situation.

Notes

1. *Casta* in Portugese signifies breed, race, or kind. Thus, *homem de boa casta* means 'a man of good family'.
2. However, when the word *biradari* is used for a caste, then it becomes an endogamous entity. Most Indians use it in this latter sense, hence the confusion.
3. *Anulom* (hypergamy) means 'with the hair', or when a girl of a lower caste is married to a boy of an upper caste. *Pratilom* (hypogamy) is just the opposite – 'against the hair', or when an upper caste girl is married to a lower caste boy.
4. I have proposed the use of this term in my book, *The Changing Frontiers of Caste*, 1968, National Publishing House, Delhi, p. 15.
5. The Brahmans of Tamil Nadu are divided into Smarthas and Shri Vaishnavas. The Smarthas are divided into Vadama, Brihacharanam, Aslasahasram, and Vattiman. Again, the Vadama are divided into Vadadesha and Chozhadesha. The term caste must be employed for the minimally endogamous group only and not for the grouping of such units. The higher groupings might indicate the past pattern of unity from which they fissured out to form distinct endogamous groups.
6. In the South, caste is not used in the name of the individual in several cases. For example, M.N. Srinivas: M stands for Mysore (his place of birth), N stands for Narasimhachar (his father's name) and it is the last name, Srinivas, which is his name and not his caste name.
7. See Yogesh Atal, *The Changing Frontiers of Caste*, 1968, National Publishing House, Delhi, Chapter 1.
8. See S. Radhakrishnan, *The Hindu View of Life,* 1954, George Allen & Unwin Ltd, London, p. 112.
9. See G.S. Ghurye, *Caste and Class in India*, 1957, Popular Book Depot, Mumbai, p. 45.
10. Despite the Kewat and the Kaibartta being people of the same origin, they are virtually different castes, separated by regional boundaries which hampered interaction between them. The Kewat are from Uttar Pradesh and the Kaibartta from West Bengal and both are endogamous units.

11. To quote Hutton, There "are still parts of India where caste is fluid enough to make it possible for persons to acquire a caste into which they were not born". (J.H. Hutton, *Caste in India*, 1961, Oxford University Press, p. 49).
12. S.C. Dube, *Indian Society*, 1990, National Book Trust, New Delhi, p. 48.
13. See M.N. Srinivas, *Social Change in Modern India*, Reprinted in 2002, Orient Longman Pvt. Ltd, New Delhi, p. 6.
14. Adrian C. Mayer, *Caste and Kinship in Central India*, 1960, Routledge and Kegan Paul, London, p. 4.

7

Marriage, Family, and Kinship

In this chapter . . .

Family is an important unit of any society. It serves as the principal group for the recruitment of new members to the society. We have seen earlier that a society acquires its new members either through birth or through immigration. For the birth of a child, it is necessary to have persons of both the sexes enjoying a marital relationship. Thus, the smallest family consists of husband and wife, and their child(ren). Without children, the couple is regarded as a 'conjugal unit', a potential family. But with the birth of a child, a conjugal unit is transformed into a 'nuclear' family.

A Mewar bridegroom surrounded by kin

Every society prescribes rules regarding marriage – who can marry whom, and among whom marriage is not permitted. Prohibition of marriage between certain individuals is called 'incest taboo'. What is incest and what is not is also culturally defined. However, in practically all the societies of the world, sexual relations between parents and children and between the siblings (children of the same parents) are regarded as incest and taboo. Beyond this, the extension of incest taboos differ from society to society, and from religion to religion. Thus, while the family is universal, the rules regarding marriage and the rules governing relationships between relatives – called kinsmen – are very different.

India is a multicultural society with the presence of several tribal groups and practitioners of different religions. Such a demographic composition makes the institution of family in India a very complex phenomenon. Families in India are both patriarchal (those in which authority flows from the father) and matriarchal (those in which authority flows from the mother). These determine rules regarding lineage and descent, residence, inheritance, and incest. Differences also exist in regard to the composition of the family. In most treatments of Indian society, which are based on Hindu scriptures, what is described as the Indian family is usually the portrayal of the 'ideal Hindu' family. Apart from the fact that the 'real' Hindu families in modern India do not correspond to the 'ideal', such portrayals fail to describe the institutions of family and marriage among other groups. It is also to be mentioned that even among the Hindus, wide variations are found in these institutions in different regions. Professor Irawati Karve was the first sociologist who contributed to our understanding of the structure of Indian society by publishing in 1953 a monumental work on the *Kinship Organization in India*.[1] Karve brought out the differences in the social system of Northern India and Southern India.

Families can be classified in several ways. The most common ways of classifying them are types of marriage, residence, size of the family, composition of the family, authority structure, and descent and inheritance. We will use these variables to identify the types of families found in India.

Families Based on Types of Marriage

Using the criterion of number of spouses, and also the premarital kinship relationship between the spouses, families can be classified as monogamous or polygamous.

A basic distinction is made between a person having one spouse or more than one spouse. The first type is called monogamy (mono = single, and 'gamy' = marriage), and it is the commonest form of marriage throughout the world, irrespective of religion or nationality. Having more than one spouse is similarly called polygamy ('poly' means plural). Polygamy is further divided into polygyny (having more than one wife) and polyandry (having more than one husband).

A man having more than one wife represents polygyny; for example, in specific circumstances, a Muslim husband is allowed to have up to four wives. It is not necessary that all the marriages take place at the same time; what is important is that the moment a person acquires a second wife through a formal marriage, his family becomes polygynous. This excludes those cases in which a person marries a second time after getting divorced or widowed; in such cases, he remains monogamous.

Polygynous families are also found among the Hindus, particularly in parts of Northern India, where a widow is remarried to the brother of her dead husband. This practice is technically called the levirate. But such a union becomes polygynous only when the husband's brother marrying the widow is already married. When this marriage takes place between the widow and the bachelor brother of the dead man, then it is only an instance of the levirate. Instances are also found of the husband marrying his wife's sister, either as a second wife, or after the death of his first wife. This practice is called the sororate. It becomes a case of sororal polygyny only when the man does not wait for the death of his wife to marry her younger sister; in such cases, both sisters share a common husband.

Polyandry is the opposite of polygyny. Families in which a woman is married to several husbands at the same time are called polyandrous. The most famous example of a polyandrous family in India is that of the Pandavas – the heroes of the *Mahabharat* – who had Draupadi as a common wife. Like the Pandavas, the husbands can be brothers making such a marriage fraternal (or adelphic) polyandry. Such forms of marriage are still to be found, although they are giving way to monogamy, amongst the Khasas of the Jaunpur-Bawar area in Uttaranchal and the Todas of the Nilgiri Hills. The Nayars of Kerala were also polyandrous.

Polyandry is also found among the Tiyan, Kota, Iravan, and the Ladakhi Bota. The Todas and the Nayars allow non-fraternal polyandry, in which the husbands of the same woman do not have to be close relatives. The wife spends her time, with each husband in turn. Among the Todas, where non-fraternal polyandry is found, the paternity of a child is determined socially. Irrespective of who the biological father of a child is, any of the husbands may accept the responsibility. In Toda society, to announce the fatherhood, the sociological father retires with his pregnant wife to the nearby jungle, where, in the presence of his tribesmen, he performs a customary bow and arrow ceremony. Such practices are needed because the Todas have a mix of matriarchal and patriarchal families – residence being maternal and inheritance paternal. This practice of the husband leading the life of an invalid along with his pregnant wife is technically called *couvade*.

In ancient times, permission was granted to a Hindu woman to have an extra-marital relationship with a person in order to beget a child to continue the family line. This was given the name of *niyoga* (appointment). Under *niyoga*, "the marital relations between the two were temporary and restricted. They lasted till the signs of pregnancy were visible or at the most ...till two children were born".[2] No privileged intimacy existed between the partners and "conjugal rights were sanctioned only to secure an heir to the deceased. That this conjugal relation was allowed only for the continuation of the line is confirmed by the fact that a widow who was either barren, or past child-bearing, or very aged was not allowed to resort to *niyoga*. Likewise, a person who was sickly was not commissioned to beget in *niyoga*" (ibid). The most famous instance is that of Bhishma, who was approached by his stepmother to marry the widows of Vichitravirya, who died childless, thus creating a crisis for the continuation of the line of Shantanu (father of Bhishma and Vichitravirya). While Bhishma found nothing wrong in her mother asking him to marry his younger brother's widows, he did not comply with the request because of his vow to remain celibate. As an alternative, he sought the services of the great sage Vyas to beget children on the widows of his stepbrother. Had Bhishma agreed to the proposal and married the widows of his brother, it would have been an instance of senior levirate. The alternative opted for was a case of *niyoga*.

Some groups also follow a pattern of preferred marriages. For example, in the South, marriage between the mother's brother (MoBr =*mama)* and his elder sister's daughter *(*SiDa = *bhanji*) is a preferred form of marriage. Similarly, marriages are also preferred with the mother's brother's daughter (MoBrDa: *mameri behn*) and the father's sister's daughter (FaSiDa: *fuferi behn)* or, which is the same thing, with the mother's brother's son (MoBrSo) and the father's sister' son (FaSiSo).[3] Both are instances of cross-cousin marriages. In technical terms, cross cousins are the children of siblings of the opposite sex. Thus, the children of FaSi and MoBr are cross-cousins. Similarly, parallel cousins are the children of siblings of the same sex. Thus, children of FaBr and MoSi are parallel cousins. See the following diagram:

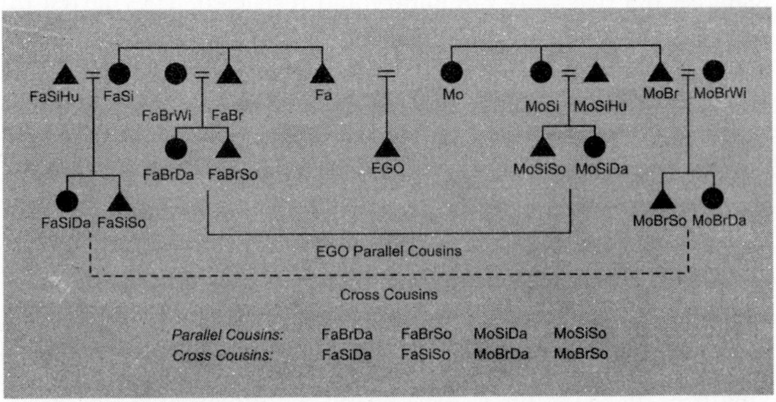

In the Hindus of South and amongst Christians and several tribal groups of India, cross-cousin marriages are generally preferred, but amongst the Hindus of Northern India, these are taboo and regarded as incest. The Muslims allow even parallel cousin marriages, along with other preferred marriages such as cross-cousin marriages and marriages between *mama* (MoBr) and *bhanji* (SiDa).

Writing about the Southern zone, Irawati Karve has enumerated the following taboos (Karve, 1965: 224):

1. A man can marry his *elder* sister's daughter, but not his *younger* sister's daughter. The Brahmans are, however, an exception to this rule.
2. Widow remarriage is allowed (except amongst Brahmans), but not the levirate. A widow cannot marry her husband's brother. This taboo is observed in Tamil Nadu, Andhra Pradesh, Karnataka, and Kerala.
3. A person is not allowed to marry his mother's sister's daughter (MoSiDa).
4. "The complicated kinship arising in a family owing to maternal-uncle-niece (MoBr with SiDa) marriages and cross-cousin marriages sometimes results in two people being related to each other in more ways than one. There may be one relationship in which a marriage would be ordinarily forbidden, while from another angle, the relationship may be one in which a marriage usually does take place."

Residence as the Basis for Family Type

Families are also classified on the basis of their residence. Broadly speaking, the couple comes to reside either with the husband's family (in patriarchal societies) or with the wife's family (in matriarchal societies). Such families are called patrilocal and matrilocal, respectively. When the couple decides to stay in a new place, it is called a neolocal residence. Some scholars also make the distinction between virilocal (husband's house) and uxorilocal (wife's house). The difference is that patrilocal and matrilocal denote the residence of the joint family, whereas virilocal and uxorilocal, as also neolocal, are the residences of the conjugal unit or the nuclear family. Instances are also found among patrilineal societies of the husband living with his wife's family, particularly when there is no male heir in the wife's family and the daughter's husband (DaHu = son-in-law) is adopted as a son, calling him a *ghar-jamai* (resident son-in-law).

This typology is used in many community studies to find the incidence of different types of families. This has been done to find particularly the extent of the joint family system. Based on these studies, it is suggested that there is a visible trend toward neolocal residences with the preponderance of the nuclear family. Because of the mobility of individuals and growing urbanization, there is a certain breakdown of the joint family in the sense that members of such units are getting dispersed in terms of residence. Consequently, there are changes in the authority structure and maintenance of family finances. However, living separately and in different communities does not mean complete severing of ties. Solidarity at the level of the joint family is exhibited in family functions and constant interactions between the dispersed units. It is for this reason that I. P. Desai concluded his analysis of the family in Mahua in Gujarat with the statement: "The joint family is dead, long live the joint family."

Family Types on the Basis of Size of Household

According to Census definitions, the word household is generally used in place of the family. They employ what they call a structural definition. Structure, in this context, refers to the physical structure of the house. All those living in the same house and sharing a common hearth are included in the definition of the family or household. Such a definition gives the idea of the size of the family, but not of its composition in terms of kinship.

The data on family size, available through Census records, are an important source for identifying changes in the family. A comparison of the average household size between 1911 and 1961 is given in the following table:

Table 1

Average Size of the Household during 1911-1961

Year	*Average size*
1911	4.6
1921	4.6
1931	4.8
1941	5.0
1951	5.0
1961	5.2

Performing family ritual

These figures indicate that the size of the household is increasing rather than decreasing. In other words, there are more persons per family today than in the beginning of the twentieth century. This signifies that while the joint family may have been the ideal form of family, in actual fact, such families were not the norm. An average size of 4.6 can include husband, wife, and two or more children – such a composition cannot qualify as a joint family. Furthermore, the data also refute the Western generalization that increasing urbanization leads to reduction in the size of the family. Henry Orenstein used the Census data from 1867 through 1951 to conclude that industrialization and Westernization have not decreased the average size of the household. Similarly, a study of Pune city by Richard Lambert also found that the average size of the family of those working in industrial enterprises was larger (5.2) compared to the average family size of the town of Pune (4.5). Again, the larger size in the industrial area need not reflect the pattern of a joint family. Other studies suggest that rural migrants in urban areas tend to accommodate fellow villagers or distant kin in their households. All these facts indicate that there is need to be cautious about vague generalizations regarding the existence, or breakdown, of the joint family in India.

Family Types Based on Composition of the Members

To get a better idea of the types of families that are currently found in our villages and towns, some students of family have carried out sample surveys of households and proposed typologies based on the kin composition of the family. A review of such empirical studies suggests that patriarchal families can be divided into seven major types. The incidence of each type may vary from community to community, but not their composition. Basically, there are two types of patriarchal families: nuclear (or simple) families and extended (or joint) families. Since the word joint is generally associated with Hindu families and the concept has legal connotations, a neutral term 'extended' is preferred by many sociologists. The other types are instances of variations of, or 'incompleteness' of the two major types.

Here is the typology of the family:

1. Nuclear (simple) family
   This consists of husband (Hu), wife (Wi) and child (ren);
2. Nuclear family with adhesions and/or adjuncts
   The adhesions are remnants of the earlier larger group, such as father or mother, or father's brother, or father's mother, unmarried brother or sister. Adjuncts are those who do not belong to the patrilineal family; these include affinal kins such as wife's mother or father, wife's brother or sister, widowed or divorced sister or daughter. Generally, such units maintain the character of nuclear families and treat the adhesions or adjuncts as temporary members of the family;
3. Compound family: A simple family becomes compound when the wife dies after the birth of children and the husband marries again. In this case, the unit will have two sets of children – one from the first wife and the other from the second wife. The presence of two sets of children makes the family a compound family. The family also becomes compound in case of a polygyny; in such cases; it and is called a polygynous compound family. If a man marries a widow with children from her first marriage, and has his own children from his first marriage, then there is a possibility of a third set of children from the union. Such a family with three sets of children is designated as a complex compound family.

The following diagram illustrates the three types.

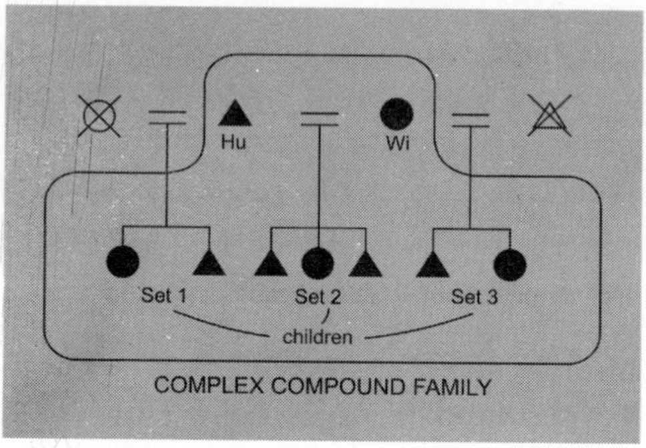

4. Incomplete Family: It is important to identify different types of incomplete families, in the sense that they do not satisfy the definition of nuclear (simple) family. A family may be incomplete due to several reasons, which may be grouped mainly under two categories:
   - (i) Breakdown of the family (may be called broken families) due to death, separation, or migration (seasonal/temporal or permanent), and
   - (ii) Initial stage of family formation, when it is only a conjugal unit. This is also called a potential nuclear family. However, if a couple is past child-bearing age, then the unit is called a nugatory nuclear family. A nugatory nuclear family can become a nuclear family with the adoption of a child.

   Another type of incomplete family is designated as a non-familial unit. Non-familial units created by breakdown may be of the following types:
   - (i) Orphaned individual;
   - (ii) Residual individual (after the death of a spouse, or upon divorce, and separation from children);
   - (iii) Dislocated unit, e.g. migrant (living alone with family left behind);

(iv) Residual conjugal unit: Husband and wife living alone after their children have separated to make their own family units, and

(v) Units with absence of a parent (incomplete nuclear families). Even in such incomplete nuclear families, there can be several patterns. For example, where the father is absent, the unit may have any of the following combinations:
Mo So (or Sons)
Mo Da (or Daughters)
Mo So Da (there can be plurality of sons or daughters, or both)

Similar patterns may be found when the mother is absent from the family, and the father has to look after the children.

There are three types of units larger than the nuclear family. These are the stem family, lineal family, and extended or joint family;

5. Stem family: A family consisting of the family of procreation of one married child linked with the ego's family of orientation in a common household is called a stem family. Such families are quite common and are often erroneously referred to as joint family. The following diagram illustrates a stem family:

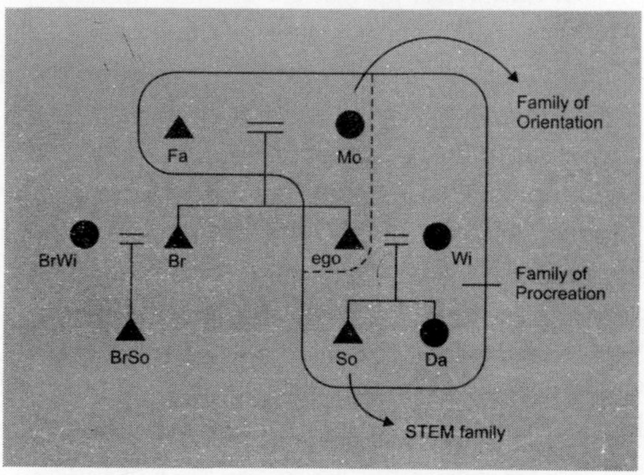

6. Lineal family: When families of procreation of several married siblings are linked to their common family of orientation, they constitute a lineal family. Such a family dissolves with the death of their parents and may become a laterally extended family or split into individual nuclear families; and

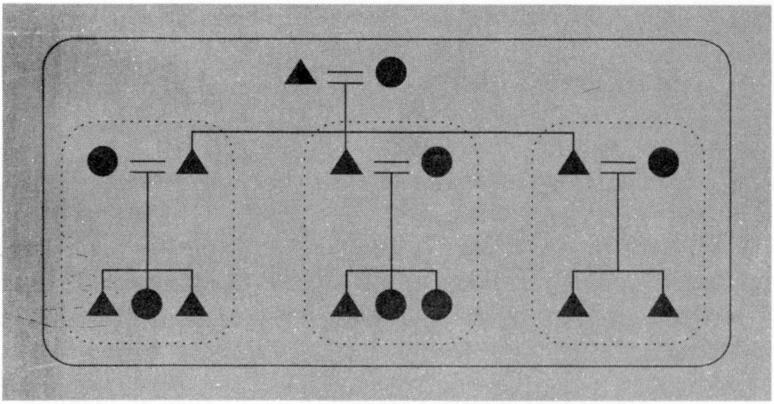

7. Extended family or joint family is one in which one can find three or more generations living together with both vertical and lateral extensions, and having a single line of authority: patrilineal or matrilineal.
Membership to such units must be distinguished from kindred, which is a bilateral kin group (though not corporate), but is composed of persons that are related – consanguineally and affinally – to a particular individual. That is why members of an individual's kindred are not all related to one another in the same manner.

Since Census data do not go beyond family size, it is difficult to say the exact incidence of each of these types of families in India and in different religious groups. But all the field studies conducted by anthropologists and sociologists in different parts of the country indicate that the number of joint or extended families, in which people of three or more generations live together and share common property, is considerably small. Such an ideal of a joint family may be one of the phases in the domestic cycle. All evidence indicates that there is greater incidence of stem and lineal families in rural India and that the number of nuclear families is on the rise in urban India. However, this does not mean complete erosion of parental authority and neglect of the older people. Family obligations do include care of old parents and solidarity on social occasions amongst the members of the extended family.

In patrilineal families, the descent is traced from the father and property is inherited from the paternal side. Women marrying into the family become members of the family clan (*gotra*) and use it as their surname; similarly, daughters move out to enter their husbands' families and change their surnames accordingly. Children born to them belong to the clan and lineage of their husbands. In royal families, inheritance follows the principle of primogeniture – the eldest son is the heir-apparent. In the absence of a son, the daughter does not automatically become the heiress. Her parents either adopt her husband or one of her sons to continue the line. In such circumstances, the daughter's son returns to the clan of her father and uses the surname of his mother's father's lineage or clan. While property is supposed to be equally distributed amongst the children, usually the married daughters do not claim or receive such inheritance. Perhaps that is one of the reasons for the prevalence of the practice of dowry and a custom of giving gifts to married daughters on all ceremonial occasions. However, the eldest brother assumes the headship of the family on the death of the father. This transfer of headship is symbolized in the turban tying ceremony held soon after the death of the father. In some areas, the eldest son starts wearing a white turban to signify his new status. In royal families, the eldest son used to escort the dead king's coffin only up to the palace gates; he had to return for his immediate coronation. Now that the institution of kingship is gone, changes are coming about in the palace culture as well. But primogeniture is still the rule.

Matrilineal Families

Since there are matrilineal families also in India, it is useful to know about them.

Matrilineal families are found in the South and in the Northeast. The Khasis of the Jayantia Hills and the Garos are the best known examples of matrilocal and matrilineal societies. The Nayars of Malabar, in Kerala, are famous both for the practice of polyandry – which is now on the decline – and matriliny. The tribe of Kadars in Kochi is also matriarchal. We shall briefly describe the family system among the Khasis, Garos, and the Nayars.

The Khasis

The Khasi family is known as an *Iing*. A typical *Iing* consists of a mother, her husband, her unmarried sons, her married daughters, their husbands and children. In matrilineal families, such as the Khasis, it is the husbands who come to stay with their wives. The male children leave upon their marriage to stay in the houses of their wives. This pattern is called matrilocal residence. The males contribute to the family income and their earnings to their mothers or to their sisters, and not to their own children, who belong to a different *Iing*. The youngest daughter is the heiress, following the principle of ultimogeniture. She acts as the priestess of the family and leads all family rituals, including the post death ceremonies that include cremation of the dead and interring of the bones into the common sepulchre (a family tomb). The elder daughters of the family are despatched to new places after their marriage. Usually, these new houses are in the same compound.

Only the youngest daughter lives in the mother's *Iing* as custodian of the house and responsible for family worship. Thus, she receives a larger share in the family property. The extended group of interconnected *Iings* is called a *kur*, a clan.

The Garo

The Garos are also matrilocal. The extended family is called a *machong*. A man leaves his *machong* after marriage to live in the *machong* of his wife. He becomes a member of her machong and adopts the name of her clan. Likewise, the children of his sister live in his mother's *machong*, and belong to her clan. The Garos also follow the principle of ultimogeniture through which the youngest daughter becomes the heiress apparent. She is called *nokna dona*. Her husband is called *nokrom*. The Husbands of the other daughters are called *chowari*. While any of the daughters can be nominated as a *nokna-dona*, it is usually the youngest

A group of Garo women (Photo by A. Playfair in 1909)

daughter who is chosen to inherit the family property. Other daughters move out to reside in separate households with their husbands. The preferred form of marriage is for a *nokna* to marry her father's sister' son (FaSiSo). In the event of the death of the nokna's father, her mother is free to marry. But if this marriage takes place, then there remains the possibility of the mother producing yet another daughter. In that case, the nokna will have to surrender her rights to the younger sister. To avoid such a crisis in the management of property, her husband, the *nokrom,* is required to marry his wife's mother (WiMo). Thus, he becomes husband at the same time of the mother and the daughter.

The Nayars

The Khasis and the Garos of the Northeast are tribal people. Many of them have adopted Christianity, but the British allowed them the practice of customary law in the matrilineal inheritance of property and descent. The Nayars of Kerala are Hindus. They are known to have allowed the practice of polyandry. It is said that matriarchy allows the possibility of polyandry in the same way as patriarchy is associated with polygyny.

The matrilocal residence of the Nayars is called a *taravad*. Unlike the Khasis and the Garos, the *taravad* did not allow the husbands of the daughters to live with them. The husbands were allowed to visit their wives in the night after dinner and leave them in the morning before breakfast. A *taravad* consists of the female members and their brothers and children. But the family authority rests with the eldest male member of the household, who is called a *karnavar*. He is allowed to bring in his wife to stay with him, but not his children, who stay with his mother's *taravad*. Marriage among the Nayars was always a loose arrangement. There are two forms of marriage among them. One is called *sambandham* and the other, *tali-kettu kalyanam*.

A Nayar woman could have a *sambandham*, not only with a member of her own caste, but also with males of higher castes of the Brahman and Kshatriya *varnas*. Such a union was formalized with the gift of clothes by the bridegroom. However, such a marriage was never binding and the woman was free to marry anyone else without any formal dissolution of the *sambandham*. The husband was not obliged to give maintenance to his divorced wife.

The *tali-kettu kalyanam* is another form of marriage, which is held before a girl attained puberty. *Tali* is a small piece of gold, which is tied by the suitor round the neck of the girl. A boy belonging to the matriclan – called *enangar* – is chosen for this ceremony. His party is received by the girl's *taravad*, the brother of the girl washes the feet of the tali-tier, after which the tali is tied. The *taravad* hosts a grand feast and the ceremony continues for four days. On the fourth day, the boy and the girl are seated in a hall or a compound where, in the presence of the village people, the girl tears off the new dress given by the bridegroom. This signifies the end of the union between the two. However, the girl observes a 15 day pollution ritual when her *tali*-tier dies. But after the *tali-kettu kalyanam* the girl is allowed to live a free life with regard to sex. She could have several visiting husbands. This is why the Nayars were called polyandrous.

Recent studies have suggested several changes in the *taravad* structure. Because of the trends of modernization and industrialization, there is greater degree of mobility. Because of this, one finds virilocal wives (wives go to reside with their husbands) and uxorilocal husbands (husbands coming to live with their wives). The factors that are responsible for virilocal residence are employment in a town, inability of the husband to visit his wife's house in a different place, poor health of the mother or the sister making it obligatory for the man to stay in his *taravad* and asking his wife to join him, etc. Similarly, uxorilocal residence is facilitated by the following factors: wife's household (called *veedu* – a smaller unit within the *taravad*) not having an elder man to run the affairs or a male kin of the wife leaving for an urban area for employment. As a result of these changes, there are now instances of children taking the name of their father and avoiding the *taravad* name. The families are now becoming a mix of matriliny and patriliny.

There is also the unique case of the Moplas, a Muslim community found both in Kerala and in the Lakshadweep and Minicoy Islands. These converts from Hinduism have carried matriliny into Islam.

As elsewhere, the family in India is also undergoing changes. The description of the 'ideal' types in different religious groups or matrilineal and patrilineal societies no longer corresponds to present-day families. There is a growing trend towards disintegration of the larger families – joint families, *taravads*, *kurs*, or *machongs*. The greater mobility enjoyed by the people has resulted in the formation of nuclear families in neolocal residences. Similarly, marriages are somewhat less restricted in terms of the preferred kin, or region or caste, or even religion. Overall, there is a broadening of the endogamous frontier. While still small, there is a trend towards intercaste marriages. Families now search for suitable spouses for their children via newspaper advertisements and even through the Internet. There is also reduction in the number of ceremonies associated with marriage and in the involvement of the wider range of kinsmen. There is also evidence to suggest that divorces are now not uncommon. However, the practice of dowry has become problematic with demands from the groom's side ever rising. Instances are often reported of dowry deaths and women being tortured and killed by their in-laws in the event of not getting the demanded dowry. Laws have been made more stringent with regard to dowry, but they do not seem to have much effect. It is the same with regard to child marriages, which have long been banned through the famous Harbilas Sarda Act of 1929; even today, child marriages do take place, particularly in Rajasthan, and the official machinery fails to stop them.

Notes

1. The second revised edition was published by Asia Publishing House, Mumbai, in 1965.
2. See K.M. Kapadia, *Marriage and Family in India*, 1966 (3rd Edition), Oxford University Press, London, p. 60.
3. In kinship analysis, eight relationships are regarded as primary and they are abbreviated to the first two letters, one capital and the other small. These relationships are: Father (Fa), Mother (Mo), Husband (Hu), Wife (Wi), Son (So), Daughter (Da), Brother (Br), and Sister (Si). The primary relations of primary relations are secondary relations, and they are designated by combining two primary abbreviations. For example, mother's sister is a primary relation of the mother, hence a secondary relation, so she is represented by MoSi. MoSiDa will, thus, become a tertiary relation.

8

Status of Women

In this chapter . . .

In our chapter on family and kinship, we talked about patriarchy and matriarchy. It was noted that the distinction between the two systems was made on the basis of the line of authority. In patriarchy, women play a subordinate role. In matriarchy the roles are reversed. The gender inequality that exists in most societies has attracted worldwide attention. The *status* of women, as compared

Old Savara woman

to men generally being lower in patriarchal systems (which are in a majority) led the world community to pledge itself to correct this social evil and fight against discrimination based on sex. The United Nations declared the year 1975 as the International Year of Women, and later the entire decade, beginning in 1976, was devoted to it.

'Status' is a sociological concept. An individual, as a member of a society, occupies a number of statuses. It is the totality of these statuses that gives the person a 'station' in the social system. Some statuses are ranked; others are common in different strata of society. For example, statuses such as mother, wife, and sister are common in all classes of society; on the other hand, statuses such as student, teacher, and principal are ranked – the principal being superior to the teacher, and the teacher being superior to the student. But in relative terms, even kinship statuses become ranked. Thus, a mother compared to a father, a wife compared to a husband, a sister compared to a brother, or siblings in terms of their age, are all ranked. When we talk of status of women we are referring to the position a woman has by virtue of her being a woman. This is different from the status of a *particular* woman as compared to *other* women. A woman of a prime minister's status is superior to her male cabinet ministers. A middle class housewife has a higher status than her domestic maid servant. In this sense, different women have different statuses. But here, we are not talking about these statuses. Our concern is to see how women *as women* are treated compared to men *as men*.

Women are regarded as the weaker section. They are regarded as weaker compared to men in social terms. But not all women are of the same status. In each society, there are rich and poor women, educated and uneducated women, rural and urban women, employed and unemployed women, women in higher positions and women in lower positions. But in every respect, women are generally seen to be lagging behind. Therefore, they come in the category of the 'backward', but they do not constitute a 'class' by themselves. We should distinguish between a category and a class. It should be said that the use of the word 'status' in the context of women is not in strict sociological terms. Common people do not make fine technical distinctions.

Most of Indian society, which is patriarchal, irrespective of religion, is characterized by male dominance. Despite the fact that in the Hindu religion, there is a strong current of goddess worship, and women are depicted as the embodiment of Shakti – moving force, power – in every day life, women are regarded as inferior to men. On the one hand, it is proclaimed that "the gods live where women are worshipped (*yatra nariyestu pujayante ramante tatra devta*)", on the other, several restrictions are imposed on women. There are stricter norms to control their sexuality, to restrict their movements, and to disallow them several property rights and other social privileges. Even today, widow remarriage is generally discouraged. The custom of Sati – a widow being burnt alive on the funeral pyre of her husband – is long banned, yet whenever such an aberration occurs, people exhibit mixed responses. In some parts of India, girls are still married in their childhood, they are confined to their homes as they grow, and they are generally denied access to education. This situation is rapidly changing, and yet its incidence is a matter of great worry.

During the British period, some legal steps were taken to improve the status of women. Banning of Sati, and child marriages were two such actions. Some Indian reformists also worked for the spread of education among women. As part of the freedom movement, Mahatma Gandhi tried to involve women in his *Satyagrah* movements and to promote literacy amongst them.[1] The Constitution of India incorporated the concept of gender equality by guaranteeing to all citizens "equality of status and opportunity ...assuring the dignity of the individual". Article 14 ensures equality before law and Article 15 "prohibits any discrimination" and makes special provisions for women and children. Preparatory to the International Women's Year in 1975, the Government of India appointed a National Committee on the Status of Women in 1971. The Committee was entrusted with the task of examining the impact of constitutional, legal, and administrative provisions on the status of women since independence. The Report came out with the following conclusions:

1. The majority of women still do not enjoy the rights and privileges guaranteed to them by the Constitution;
2. A favourable environment does not exist for women to play the multiple roles they are expected to play;
3. Increasing incidence of practices like dowry indicates a further lowering of the status of women;
4. The concern for women and their problems, which received an impetus during the freedom movement, has suffered a decline; and

5. Women are generally ignorant of their legal rights.

The Committee made the following observations with regard to the status of women in India:

1. Equality of women is necessary not merely on the grounds of social justice, but as a basic condition for the social, economic, and political development of the nation;
2. Improvement of employment opportunities and earning power is essential to free women from their economic dependence;
3. Safe bearing and rearing of children is an obligation that should also be shared by the father, the family, and society at large.
4. The contribution made by an active housewife to the running and management of a family should be regarded as economically and socially productive;
5. Marriage and motherhood should not become a disability in women's fulfilling their role in the task of national development;
6. Any policy or movement for the emancipation and development of women has to form a part of a total movement for the removal of inequalities and oppressive social institutions; and
7. Effective steps should be taken to transform *de jure* equality into *de facto* equality.

Since 1975, when the National Committee submitted its report to the Government of India, several steps have been taken to improve the condition of women. A large number of studies have been carried out under the auspices of the Indian Council of Social Science Research to investigate different aspects of the problem of gender equality. Many universities have also introduced courses on women's studies. UNESCO has encouraged the preparation of teaching materials and commissioned a few studies relative to family, participation of women in politics, women decision makers, women in the informal sector, and violence against women.

As part of the programme of human resource development, emphasis is given to the development of the full potential of women and children. In 1985, the Ministry of Human Resource Development set up a Department of Women and Child Development (DWCD). Under this department, there are two bureaus – for Women's Development and Women's Welfare, respectively. The Department has also created two autonomous organizations especially for women. These are the National Commission for Women (NCW) and the Rashtriya Mahila Kosh (RMK).

The National Commission for Women was constituted in 1992 following the Act passed by Parliament in 1990. The Central government nominates its chairperson, five members, and a member-secretary. The Commission is mandated to review legislation and intervene in specific cases of atrocities against women and denial of their rights.

The Rashtriya Mahila Kosh (RMK), also called The National Credit Fund for Women, was set up in March 1993 with a corpus fund of Rs 31 crore to provide small credit to poor women working in the informal sector.

To get an idea of the continuing disparities, we shall briefly examine female literacy, female participation in the economy, legal aid, and women in political and public life.

Sex Ratio

We should first take a look at the demographic profile of India.

As we have seen earlier, the Census of India 2001 put the population of India at 1,027 million people. Of this population, women constitute 495.7 million, or 48.2 per cent of the total population. This means that the number of women is less than

Table 1
Sex Ratio: 1901-2001

Census Year	*Sex Ratio (Females per 1,000 Males)*
1901	972
1911	964
1921	955
1931	950
1941	945
1951	941
1961	930
1971	934
1981	934
1991	927
2001	933

half the total population. Although the sex ratio has always been unfavourable to women, its continuous decline is a cause for worry. In 1901 – a century ago – the sex ratio was 972 women per 1,000 men. This has come down to 933 in 2001, which is a slight improvement on the 1991 figure of 927.[2] It will be useful here to present in a tabular form the declining sex ratio since 1901.

As sociologists, we are not interested in just numbers. Our focus is on investigating the cause for this decline and also on studying the social consequences of such a demographic composition. Students of polyandry, for example, found a relationship between the sex ratio and the marital practice. When the numbers are not equal, there is bound to be a shortage of spouses. Going into the causes, it is found that the high priority given to the male child in patrilineal societies has led to practices such as female infanticide and neglect of the girl child in the family. The high dowry demands and incidence of domestic violence against women have also contributed to the general dislike for a female child. With the relaxation of laws regarding abortion, people are motivated to use sonography for sex determination and getting the pregnancy terminated in the event of the embryo being female. High maternal mortality also disturbs the sex ratio.

A region-wise analysis of sex ratio given by the Census tells us a disturbing story. While the average sex ratio for India as a whole is 933, it is as low as 861 in Haryana and 874 in the Punjab. In the Union territory of Chandigarh, it is only 773, and in Daman and Diu, it is 709. There are 18 states in the Indian Union where the sex ratio is below the national average. This certainly is a cause for worry and calls for effective policy measures to curb this trend. It is in this context that medical practitioners have been asked to stop the use of sonography for sex determination. Efforts are also being made to improve the nutritional status of females and to expand maternity and child health services to improve female life expectancy.

Literacy and Education

Education is regarded as a key instrument for the empowerment of women. Education changes their worldview, improves their chances of employment, facilitates their participation in public life, and also influences their fertility. Several studies indicate that educated women have, on an average, fewer children and they take good care of their socialization.

Although considerable progress has been made with regard to literacy and education, the overall picture still remains unfavourable to women. At the beginning of the 20th century, the country as a whole was largely illiterate with just 5.3 per cent of the population counted as literate. Only 0.60 per cent women were then literate. In 1951, the first Census taken four years after independence, the picture was not much better. The female literacy rate stood at 7.93 per cent, as compared to 24.95 per cent for men. The 2001 Census suggests a 65.38 per cent literacy rate for India, with 75.85 per cent for males, and 54.16 per cent for females. Literacy is not evenly spread throughout India. There are 12 states and Union territories that are below the national average for female literacy. The states of Bihar and Jharkhand have the lowest female literacy rates (33.57 and 39.38%, respectively). These data suggest that nearly half of India's female population is still illiterate. This is not a small number. A massive programme is needed to make nearly 240 million women literate. It is also to be noted that most of these women are located in rural and tribal areas. Another point to remember is that most of the women included in the literate category have not had education beyond the primary level. The number of women goes down as we move to higher levels of education. However, women are to be found in all professions, including medicine and engineering. An idea can, however, be had by knowing the percentage of females by number of years of schooling. The 1991 figures for educational composition of women, in terms of number of years of schooling, is given below:

Table 2
Educational Composition of Women by Number of Years of Schooling in 1991

Number of Years of Schooling	*Total Population*	*Female*
No Education or Less than 3 Years	56.7	68.4
3-6 Years	23.7	19.3
7-11 Years	11.0	7.1
12-14 Years	6.8	4.2
15+ Years	1.8	1.0

The *1998 Year Book* of the Institute of Applied Manpower Research provides figures regarding the enrolment of girls by

Table 3
Enrolment of Girls by Stages of Education

(Figures in Thousands)

Stage	*1961*	*1971*	*1981*	*1991*	*1997*
A. General Education					
Pre-Primary	82	168	5 23	745	1,115
Primary	10,944	21,306	28,488	40,420	47,892
Middle	1,941	3,889	6,790	12,439	16,359
High/Higher Secondary	687	1,708	2,650	4,749	6,628
Post-Matric but Below Degree Level	94	228	834	2,032	3,164
Degree and above	354	396	689	1,264	1,997
B. Professional/Tech./ Vocational Education					
School Level	101	109	155	NA	NA
Post-Matric but Below Degree Level	–	81	111	NA	NA
Degree and Above	33	51	110	173	NA

Note: Adapted from IAMR *Yearbook 1998,* Table 2.1.7, page 85.

stages of education. These are reproduced in Table 3 which suggests that only 77.15 million girls were enrolled as students in different courses. The male enrolment figure was much higher - 109 million. Of course, over the years, the gap between boys and girls with regard to enrolment is getting smaller and smaller, but there is still need to accelerate the process of universalization of education among women. Simultaneously, there is also a need to take measures to reduce the dropout rate, which is fairly high, particularly among village girls.

The government realizes the importance of education in bringing about basic change in the status of women. Initially, the policy thrust was on welfare, which changed to development in the 1980s, and is now redefined as empowerment. Education is seen as a major contributor to the empowerment process. In this regard, the following programmes undertaken by the government deserve special mention:

1. *Mahila Samakhya:* Started in 1989, this scheme uses education as a tool for empowerment. This scheme is being carried out in 8,000 villages in 53 districts in the states of Andhra Pradesh, Assam, Bihar, Gujarat, Karnataka, Kerala, Madhya Pradesh, and Uttar Pradesh.
2. *Sarva Shiksha Abhiyan:* This is a campaign to universalise primary education, as part of the international programme of Education For All (EFA). It is inspired by UNESCO's regional programme called APPEAL – Asia Pacific Programme of Education for All.

In addition, there are other programmes of the Ministry of Human Resource Development, which also cover women's education. These include Operation Blackboard, Non-Formal Education, District Primary Education Programme, National Literacy Mission, Navodaya Vidyalaya, and Vocational Education. In the state of Rajasthan, which has low rates of literacy among rural and tribal women, an innovative programme called Lok Jumbish was launched with financial assistance from the Swedish International Development Authority (SIDA) in 1992. This programme was, however, closed down in 2004.

Employment

It is a general belief that economic dependence of women is a major obstacle to their empowerment. Women's participation in the labour force is, therefore, regarded as an index of their empowerment. It is believed that economic independence gives them personal autonomy and the power of decision making. Studies have shown that a decline in their employment adversely affects their fertility, mortality, and nutrition. Viewed from this

Women at work

angle, women of the lower strata can be considered as empowered because most of them work as labour, not only in their private homes, but also as paid workers – maid servants, labour on daily wages, and women employed in salaried jobs – both skilled and non-skilled. But there is also a sizeable number of women who are out of the labour force. Not all of them, however, enjoy a low status in society. D.R. Gadgil made a very interesting point in this regard: "The ability to keep away from manual work has been an important distinguishing sign of socioeconomic status among us. Therefore, non-participation of women in any work, and particularly manual work outdoors, is considered a value…"[3] From this angle, all non-working women cannot be considered as poor or deprived of high status. Non-work in such cases gives them a high status.

Employment data indicate that there has been marked difference in the work participation rates of males and females in India. Until 1961, female participation rate was nearly half the male rate. But in 1971, the female rate declined considerably as compared to the male rate (14.2% for females and 52.8% for males). The Census of 1971 reported 31 million women in the labour force, of which 28 million were from the rural areas, representing only 13 per cent of the total rural female population eligible for the labour force. As against this, only 7 per cent of the urban women – 3 million – participated in the work force. These figures were disputed by the Planning Commission on the ground of the definition employed for workforce participation. According to the Planning Commission, the rate in 1971 was 28 per cent. In 1981, the female workforce was calculated at 66.3 million, with a female participation rate of 20.85 per cent – higher than in the 1971 Census, but again lower than the Planning Commission estimates. The 1981 figures suggest that the largest number (46%) of women workers were agricultural labourers. This proportion has increased from 24.6 in 1961 to 46 per cent in 1981. An analysis of the 1981 data suggested that women began to lose their traditional avenues and did not get absorbed in the modern sectors. A small section of middle class educated women benefited from developmental activities by getting administrative jobs. The 1993-94 data on the workforce participation rate suggests that the rates for rural women is 32.8 per cent (representing 92 million women) and for urban women, 15.5 per cent (representing 17.3 million women). Thus, there were 109.3 million women in the workforce as compared to 251.1 million men.

Women workers are found both in the organized and unorganized sectors. Some estimates suggest that 94 per cent of women are employed in the unorganized sector. In the organized sectors, they are generally employed in factories, mines, and plantations. There is also a steady growth of female workers in the services and professions. In the latter, it is the teaching and nursing profession that has attracted women. In 1993-94, 56.7 per cent women in the labour force were self-employed, 6.3 per cent were regular employees, and 37 per cent were casual labour. Since women work in the unorganized sector, they are not covered by protective laws and policies. They possess poor skills, get low wages, face job insecurity, and are subjected to different types of exploitation. Women are, thus, a vulnerable group. Uneducated women find it difficult to get better paid jobs, and in the highly competitive job market, even the educated women remain unemployed. Education does not necessarily lead to employment.

Some legal measures have been taken to correct the situation. The Equal Remuneration Act of 1976 requires that employers pay the same wages to men and women doing the same or similar work. The Maternity Benefit Act of 1961 provides for paid leave up to a maximum of 12 weeks. The Employees State Insurance Act also has provisions for maternity benefits. There are other Acts that prohibit employment of women between 7 pm and 6 am in factories, mines, and plantations. Some rules regulate working hours for women, put conditions on the amount of weight to be lifted by them, and prescribe norms for their safety and welfare.

Social Legislation

Age at Marriage

As was said earlier, there was a practice among the Hindus – still prevalent in some parts – to marry off girls before the attainment of puberty. This led to child marriages, early pregnancies, maternal deaths, poor health of women, and a larger incidence of young widows. While the upper caste Hindus disallowed widow remarriages, the men were free to remarry.

As early as 1891 an Act was passed, under which consummation of marriage was prevented before the age of 12 years for a girl. However, this could not be enforced, and in 1929, the Child Marriage Restraint Act was passed, which is better known as the Sarda Act, after the name of Harbilas Sarda who campaigned for it. Girls below the age of 14 years and boys below the age of 18 years were banned from marriage. Though such marriages were not invalidated, the Act had provisions for punishment of those responsible for bringing them about. This Act was applicable to all, irrespective of religion. The Hindu Marriage Act of 1955 raised the minimum age for marriage to 15 years for the girl. But again, marriages violating the Act were only punishable by a 15 days' simple imprisonment, or a fine of up to Rs 1,000. Subsequently, these Acts have been amended further raising the age at marriage for girls to 18 and for boys to 21.

Dowry

Dowry is defined as any property or valuable security that passes directly or indirectly between the parties to the marriage at, before, or after the marriage as consideration for the marriage. According to the Dowry Prohibition Act of 1961, giving, taking, or even demanding dowry is punishable with imprisonment of up to six months or a fine of up to Rs 5,000, or both. In case of a dowry death, a dying statement is considered good enough evidence to convict the offender. The 1961 Act has been made stricter. However, the menace of dowry continues to ruin many lives. Some women's groups are actively working for the abolition of the dowry system.

Divorce

While divorce and widow remarriage were prevalent among the so-called lower castes, these were not allowed among the upper castes. As a result of *Sanskritization*, many lower caste people also gave up these practices to climb up in the ritual hierarchy of castes. But with the changing times, these rules have been relaxed. Reformist movements have worked to promote widow remarriages and legal measures have been taken to allow divorce among the Hindus. Among the Muslims, Christians, and other groups, however, no such restrictions existed. Under the Hindu law, divorce can be sought by either of the spouses on grounds of adultery, desertion, cruelty, unsound mind, venereal disease, leprosy, mutual consent, and either partner not being heard of as being alive for a period of at least seven years. Additionally, a wife can ask for a divorce if the husband marries a second time (bigamy) or is convicted for rape, sodomy, or bestiality.

Women in Politics

Women's participation in politics is still not very impressive. The number of women politicians is small as compared to men. The majority of women are indifferent to politics; this is clear in their low participation in voting, in public demonstrations, and in public debates. Whatever participation there is it is mostly limited to women from the urban elite groups. Some of the studies suggest that women see politics as a power game of the well-to-do. The poorer women are more preoccupied with daily bread issues rather than the broader questions of women's development and national politics. It is interesting that a higher voting percentage is found among rural and poor women, while the urban and the educated show a poor polling turnout. Thus, participation in voting cannot be regarded as a reliable indicator of political awareness. Women vote on the instructions of their men and, at times, because their votes are bought by political competitors. Sushila Kaushik is of the view that despite these developments, the following can be said about women's participation in politics in India:

1. The extent, nature, and level of Indian women's participation is much greater than in many countries;
2. This participation has been more or less steadily expanding over the years through various elections – as voters, as candidates, and in terms of participation in campaigning, etc.;
3. The gap in turnout between men and women is increasingly narrowing down; and
4. The number of women getting elected to representative bodies is steadily increasing.[4]

Because of legislation, there is now greater representation of women in village panchayats and local bodies. Some of these bodies are even headed by women. But it is alleged that these women are only figureheads and the real power is wielded by their husbands for whom they stand proxy.

All political parties feel the necessity of increasing the number of women parliamentarians and legislators. In this regard, a draft Bill suggesting a reservation of 33 per cent of seats for women is pending in Parliament. There is lack of consensus about the modality to ensure such representation. In the recent elections held in the country, none of the political parties put up as many candidates, and neither the Lok Sabha – the House of the People – nor any of the state legislatures reached anywhere near the 33 per cent level. The number of women ministers is also very small. However, the country can boast of having had, in the past a woman prime minister (Indira Gandhi), and several chief ministers (Sucheta Kripalani, Nandini Satpathy, J. Jayalalitha Rabri Devi, Vasundhara Raje for example).

To conclude, it can be said that the position of women in India has improved in the last few decades. Of course, because of the spread of the mass media network, more instances of atrocities against women come to light, but it would be wrong to conclude that the incidence of violence against women has risen.

Women on the political front

This is, however, not to condone those who indulge in socially disgraceful acts against women.

Notes

1. See Nayar, Sushila, and Kamla Mankekar (eds), *Women Pioneers in India's Renaissance*, 2002, National Book Trust, New Delhi.
2. The world average is 986. Countries like the US, Indonesia, Brazil, the Russian Federation, Japan, and Nigeria have a favourable sex ratio of more than 1,000 – ranging between 1,140 and 1,004.
3. D.R. Gadgil, *Women in the Working Force in India,* 1965, Asia Publishing House, Mumbai, p. 7.
4. Susheela Kaushik, 'Women in Politics in India', in *Women in Politics*, edited by Yogesh Atal and Latika Padgaonkar, 1993, RUSHSAP Series of Monographs and Occasional Papers # 36, UNESCO, Bangkok, Chapter 2, p. 59.

9

Indian Polity

In this chapter . . .

India is the world's largest democracy. It is the only country in Asia that has remained democratic ever since it attained its independence from British rule. The only exception to this is the brief period of the Emergency in 1975-76, when the democratic process was halted. But it is through the democratic route of elections that the ruling caucus was dethroned and an alternative government installed. But that did not last long and the Congress party returned to power by winning back the confidence of the people.

Many in the world were apprehensive of the success of democracy in India. Their belief was further strengthened when several countries in the region, including Pakistan, failed as democracies and chose an authoritarian and militarist path in its stead. But this did not happen in India, and we have crossed more than half a century as a democracy. India has falsified all the prophecies of doom. It is the ballot, and not the bullet, that reigns supreme in India.

India after Independence

After a long and difficult freedom struggle, India attained her independence from British rule in 1947. But this independence came with the partition of the country. A new state of Pakistan was created with portions of Western and Eastern India, taken away from the Indian map. West Pakistan took away Western Punjab, Sindh, and Baluchistan; East Pakistan was created with the partition of Bengal into East and West, the latter remaining with India. Thus, there was a long corridor of India that separated East Pakistan from West Pakistan. That such a formation of the new state was non-pragmatic and unworkable was proven by later events. In 1971, East Pakistan broke its ties with the Western wing and became the separate country of Bangladesh. The subcontinent, which was once a single country, was divided into three nations. Meanwhile, the state of Sikkim, which was a separate kingdom ruled by the Chogyal monarchy, joined the Indian Union in 1975.

Independence arrived in India not only with 'multiplicity of heritages and legacies', but also with the pangs of partition that caused dislocation of populations on both sides. Several Muslim families from regions other than those that went to Pakistan

A Muslim woman casting vote

decided to opt for the nationality of the new religious state and to migrate there, and numerous Hindu families from both East and West Pakistan got uprooted and came to India as homeless refugees. This movement of people was not peaceful. There was a lot of bloodshed, looting, rape of women, and merciless killing of innocent people.

After the creation of Bangladesh, several Muslim families, which migrated from Bihar and other adjoining states to the Eastern wing of Pakistan, suffered from similar discrimination and marginalization. India has become a shelter for several Bangladeshis who have crossed the porous border illegally and settled in several cities of India. Their arrival in Assam, for example, caused serious problems and prompted the natives to raise the demand for repatriation of the non-Assamese. Speakers of Bengali and followers of Islam cannot be easily classified foreigners in the pluricultural society of India. Vote-bank politics has also helped in blurring their identities.

India inherited the legacy of British rule – a system of administration, an army, and a democratic form of government, based on the Government of India Act of 1935. Most important was the fact that our country retained the name India, that is Bharat. We remain the mainland, while the other states are historically the breakaway groups.

The transition from a colonial country to an independent nation was not easy. Partition entailed division of resources, transfer of government personnel from one country to another, and reorientation of the bureaucracy.

As Paul R. Brass says: "In some ways, it is possible to view Independence and the adoption in the early years after Independence of a new Constitution as another stage in the evolution of India toward representative government in a process that dates back to the Indian Councils Act of 1861 and continues through the Morley-Minto Reforms of 1909, the Montagu-Chelmsford Reforms of 1919, and the Government of India Act of 1935."[1] But the new Constitution, which was adopted by the Constituent Assembly on 26 November 1949, and came into force on 26 January 1950, has some new features, providing a sharp break with the British colonial past. It adopted the Westminster model of parliamentary government as against the mixed parliamentary-bureaucratic authoritarian system inherited from British India. The new Constitution included a chapter on Fundamental Rights, and also on Directive Principles, which were not there in the 1935 Act. The introduction of adult suffrage was also a new feature. The Indian polity became a mix of the unitary and federal forms of government.

The new leadership was equally interested in bringing about socio-economic reforms for which the model of a 'socialistic pattern of society' was adopted. The contradiction thus introduced between civil liberties and governmental control has been a subject of political protests. In addition to fundamental rights, the Constitution made special provisions for the oppressed castes and tribes by listing them in a Schedule, and thus designating them as scheduled castes (SCs) and scheduled tribes (STs).

The British divided Indian society along religious lines by creating separate electorates, as part of their policy of 'divide and rule'. But the new leadership of independent India discarded this colonial practice. However, there was unanimity on giving special protection and privileges to the scheduled castes and scheduled tribes, who had allegedly suffered from discrimination at the hands of the upper caste Hindus, and who constitute the majority of India's poor.

Designating the new state as *secular* was meant to convey the message that the country would not differentiate between people on the basis of religion, but allow each individual, as part of his/her fundamental right, to practice the religion of his/her choice. This was to ensure that communalism would be contained. However, the history of the country since independence has been witness to several communal riots and the growth of political parties along religious lines.[2] Even the so-called secular parties contributed – perhaps unintentionally – to the prevailing communal hiatus. In their enthusiasm to protect the minority groups, the secular parties became in fact promoters of communal interests in the hope of creating vote-banks. It led to a reaction amongst the majority group of Hindus. The role of the Rashtriya Swayamsewak Sangh (RSS) and the Vishwa Hindu Parishad (VHP) in promoting solidarity amongst the Hindus is seen in this political context. These non-political organizations lent their support to the Bharatiya Jan Sangh in the early days of independence, and later to its successor, the Bharatiya Janata Party (BJP).

The Indian polity in reality, and not as seen in constitutional terms, is characterized by a mix of tradition and modernity. The formal structure adopted in the Constitution has continually been modified by the social structure of Indian society, and by the personality profiles of India's political leadership. It is not the ideology, but the personality factors, that have led to the formation and dissolution of parties. Review of party manifestos issued during elections and the Common Minimum Programmes (CMPs) adopted by successive coalition governments suggests that there was little ideological distance between parties.[3] Political distance is maintained despite ideological proximity.

The actually existing political structure has departed from the ideal as perceived by the founding fathers of our Constitution. Several amendments made to the Constitution[4] tell that story, but only partially. There is nothing unusual in this. All living societies continually change in response to the emerging new demands and by the behaviour of its members in their different statuses and role relationships.

In the earlier phases, there were pressures from the rulers of princely states and owners of feudal estates seeking redefined roles as leaders in a functioning democracy. They entered politics by joining either the ruling Congress Party or the newly created Bharatiya Jan Sangh and the Swatantra Party (now defunct). But as long as the nationalist leaders who took part in India's freedom struggle were there to run the government, there was no threat to the Congress Party. The opposition remained in the minority, but was quite vocal in its criticism in Parliament and the state legislatures.

The vote politics that requires numbers led both the ruling party and the dissident groups within it, as well as the parties in the opposition, to create vote-banks by invoking caste sentiments. Caste entered politics in the sense that there was, and is, politicization of caste. In this framework, even the minorities were seen as a 'caste' – the defining characteristic of endogamy applies to them as well. If some political parties tried to woo the voters from a particular caste – Lodhis or Rajputs, or Brahmins[5]– others tried to woo the minority groups. One also notices a strange pattern of bringing together Muslims and the Hindu community of Yadavs, and other so-called Dalits. While this grouping is based on sectarian considerations, it is called secular. But a coalition of castes from the Hindu and Jain and Sikh groups is decried as anti-secular. In retort, the latter call the former 'pseudo-secular'. In this process, words like secular and secularism have lost their originally intended meaning.[6] All parties realize that no community or group can be neglected if one were to muster political support. The secular parties cannot afford to neglect the Hindu vote, and the parties that are called anti-secular also have representatives of communities other than the Hindu. All parties, barring religion based organizations, claim to be secular.

Indian politics is characterized by an absence of ideology. Only lip service is paid to ideology. Parties are dominated by personalities. Leaders don't leave and join parties on ideological grounds. Even the group of Marxists is divided into several parties. To quote Brass, "Indian politics has been characterized by an all-pervasive instrumentalism which washes away party manifestoes, rhetoric, and effective implementation of policies in an unending competition for power, status, and profit."[7]

The Congress party started as a movement that was joined by people from all sections; its sole aim was to oust the British and establish Swaraj. After the attainment of that aim, Mahatma Gandhi proposed dissolution of the Congress, but it was shot down. The euphoria of independence was so overwhelming, and the leaders of the movement so respected by the common man, that the Congress party appeared to be the natural heir to the throne. Leaders defecting from the Congress party formed most other parties later.

Students of democracy know that its proper functioning requires an opposition. In the United States, for example, there are two parties – Democratic and Republican – between whom power alternates. But in India, continuance of the Congress rule with no threat of its replacement gave rise to, what came to be known as one-party dominant system. People found this system similar to that of the Soviet state. This system fulfilled the requirement of the democratic process by creating internal dissensions within the Congress party itself. These were referred to as the 'ruling group' and the 'dissident group', and power, particularly at the level of the states, alternated between these groups, but remained with the Congress.

But India's political situation is changing. This change is taking place on several frontiers. Let us briefly mention the major changes in Indian polity that have occurred since 1947.

Division of the Indian Union into States

When India became independent, it was divided into 560 principalities, besides those provinces that were part of British India. These were of different sizes – some even larger than major European countries; they were also at different levels of development – from modernized regions to mediaeval monstrosities. All the princely states, other than that of Kashmir, Junagarh, and Hyderabad, immediately acceded to India. But they also finally joined the Indian Union. With their merger, the country was divided into A, B, and C states. Around 216 states merged as Part A states, 275 states were integrated into new administrative units called Part B states, and 61 states were put in the category of Part C states, which were Centrally governed. The heads of Part A states were called governors or *Rajyapal*s, those of Part B states, *Rajpramukhs* (with the sole exception of Rajasthan, where a higher category of *Maharajpramukh* was created to accommodate the Maharana of Mewar. But that was only a titular position; the *Maharajpramukh* never went to the state capital, Jaipur, and the position was abolished soon after the death of the incumbent Maharana[8]), and those of Part C, commissioners or lieutenant-governors.

The Union was reorganized again in November 1956 on linguistic grounds – dropping out the distinctions of A, B, and C. With this reorganization, the country was divided into 14 states and six Union territories. Further changes occurred with the separation of Gujarat and Maharashtra, the creation of Nagaland, the division of Punjab into Punjab and the Haryana, and incorporation of Goa, Daman, and Diu, when they were freed from Portuguese occupation. In November 2000, three new states were created: Uttaranchal was separated from Uttar Pradesh, Jharkhand from Bihar, and Chhattisgarh from Madhya Pradesh. Through a Constitutional amendment in Parliament, the Union territory of Delhi is now called the National Capital Territory of Delhi from 1 February 1992. The first general elections to the legislative assembly of the National Capital Territory were held in November 1993.

The Indian Union today consists of 28 states and six Union territories and the National Capital Territory (NCT) of Delhi.

Changing Party Structure

From the beginning, India remained a multi-party system. In 1952, when the first general elections were held, as many as 192 political parties were in the fray. However, the Election Commission provided election symbols to only 14 all-India parties and 52 state parties. These numbers went on changing with the formation of new parties, merger of some others, and death of several others. When the last elections for Parliament were held in 2004, there were six national parties, 45 state parties, and 730 registered but 'unrecognized' parties.

Writing in 1967, Rajni Kothari said, "The Indian system can be described as a 'one-party dominant system' (which, it may be noted, is very different from what is generally known as a one-party system). It is a competitive party system, but one in which the competing parties play rather dissimilar roles."[9]

Analysing the 1967 situation, Yogesh Atal had proposed a typology of political parties along six dimensions as shown below: regional: national; communal: secular; stable: fluctuating; old:

new; leader-dominated: interest-dominated; and clear ideology: diffused ideology. Combining these variables, a complicated typology can be created. But it can be said that even today, all the political parties can be classified along these dichotomies. In the present-day context, political leaders generally talk of secular and non-secular parties, or of national and regional parties. However, the so-called secular parties do not have much in common other than a confrontation with the non-secular or communal parties. Divided into two major groups, the talks of creating a third front or forum are quite frequent.

Independent India has seen the birth and death of many parties. Some of the parties that were active in the earlier years have disappeared from the scene either through mergers or splits. This has happened with many socialist parties. The Communist Party has also split into several Marxist or leftist parties. Even the rightist party, originally named the Bharatiya Jan Sangh, has undergone significant changes in terms of its alliances with other parties and non-political organizations. Some of the split groups from the national parties have emerged as regional parties in reality, though giving the impression of being national.

The Congress party itself got divided into the Congress (I) and Congress (O) – the 'I' standing for Indira and the 'O' for Organization. The fact that one group was named after its leader suggests the role of personalities. In recent times, the Congress (I) got split into the Trinamool Congress, led by Mamata Banerjee, and the Nationalist Congress Party (NCP), led by Sharad Pawar. It is important to note that both these groups have retained the appellation, Congress, in their new nomenclature to indicate their pedigree. It also gives the impression that such splinter parties might re-merge into the parent party after their differences are amicably resolved. The two parties that broke away from the Congress have a limited following. The Trinamool Congress has virtually become a regional party in West Bengal. Similarly, the NCP is more effective in Maharashtra – the state of its founder,

Sharad Pawar. Both at the Centre and in Maharashtra, the NCP is part of the alliance led by the Congress party.

Responding to the call made by Jayaprakash Narayan during the period of the Emergency, all opposition political parties (barring the communists) agreed to join a common front, shedding their differences. Five political parties joined the common platform to fight the 1977 elections. These were: the Congress (O), Jan Sangh, Socialist Party, Bharatiya Lok Dal, and the Congress for Democracy. Of these, three were breakaway groups from the Congress: Congress (O), led by Morarji Desai; Bharatiya Lok Dal, led by Chaudhary Charan Singh; and Congress for Democracy, led by Jagjivan Ram. All three leaders were Congress stalwarts and eager to become the Prime Minister of India. Morarji Desai and Charan Singh fulfilled their personal ambitions and became prime ministers, although for brief spells. At the time of the 1977 elections, the newly formed Janata Party could not get official recognition. Therefore, the candidates drawn from these groups fought the elections under the banner of the Bharatiya Lok Dal. After the elections, the Janata Party was formalized, but the constituents maintained their individual identities. This collective strength of the opposition succeeded in routing the Congress in the 1977 elections.

But this experiment was a short interlude. The parties joining this group could not evolve a common ideology. Internal dissensions led to the downfall of the Janata government in 1979. In April 1980, Bharatiya Jan Sangh came out of this membership and revived its organization under the new name of the Bharatiya Janata Party (BJP). The new nomenclature signified a change in the party's instance. It retained the prefix, Bharatiya, from Jan Sangh, and added it to Janata Party. It also dropped the word, 'Sangh', in favour of 'Party'. Observers felt that this was to show some distance from the RSS, as was the case in its earlier incarnation.

The remainder of the group was renamed the Janata Dal. But it got divided into several parties. Mulayam Singh set up a new socialist party, named the Samajvadi Party. But this is now virtually a regional party in Uttar Pradesh. Similarly, Lalu Prasad Yadav formed his own party, the Rashtriya Janata Dal (RJD), but again this remained confined to Bihar and Jharkhand. Ram Vilas Paswan created his own Lok Jan Shakti Party with a limited following. George Fernandes formed the Samata Party with a strong base in Bihar. The remainder of the Janata Party also got divided into JD (U) and JD (S).

There are some political parties that are basically regional, but influence national politics as well. These are the AIADMK and DMK in Tamil Nadu led by J. Jayalalithaa and Karunanidhi respectively, the Telugu Desam Party (TDP) of Andhra Pradesh, led by Chandra Babu Naidu, and the Akali Dal in Punjab. The Bahujan Samaj Party is also basically a party with a regional character, being most effective in Uttar Pradesh, where its leader, Mayawati, has reigned twice as chief minister.

Emergence of Coalition Politics

The 1967 elections – the fourth in the series – saw for the first time a real challenge to the Congress party. While it gained the majority in the Lok Sabha, it lost in several state assemblies. That was the first time when the phenomenon of tandem voting got a jolt. People voted differently for the Vidhan Sabha and the Lok Sabha.

It must be noted that even the Congress party never ever got more than 47.78 per cent votes in any Lok Sabha election, including the first one held in 1952. And this percentage came down to 40.73 in 1967. Even with less than 50 per cent support, the Congress party was able to garner more than 68 per cent of the seats in the Lok Sabha until 1967, when it won only 279 of the

521 seats, bringing down the percentage of seats to 53 per cent. 1967 can be regarded as a real turning point in the history of Indian polity, as this was when the hegemony of the ruling party was challenged.

Soon after this election, the Congress party split in 1969. The fifth elections were held in 1971, and the Congress party again registered a massive victory. This was attributed to the so-called 'Indira wave'. The 1969 split in the Congress discredited the old guard leaders – known as the syndicate – and people got enchanted with the slogan of Garibi Hatao. The quick downfall of the non-Congress governments in many states went in favour of the Congress party, impressing upon the electorate that there was no viable alternative to the Congress.

With the death of Indira Gandhi, the situation changed. While the sympathy vote made her son – Rajiv Gandhi – the prime minister, internal factions soon led to his downfall. It was during this period that the politics of coalition replaced the one-party dominant system, although the seeds for it were sown during Indira Gandhi's time.

Coalition politics now characterize the Indian polity. There is no party at the all-India level that can claim to enjoy a full majority. Even P.V. Narasimha Rao's government was formed when the Congress did not have absolute majority. With the Common Minimum Programme, the group led by the Bharatiya Janata Party (BJP) formed the government after the 1999 elections; the coalition was called the NDA, the National Democratic Alliance. The present government, headed by the Congress party is also a coalition government under the alliance called the UPA, the United Progressive Alliance. The UPA also receives support from the Marxist group of parties, which have refused to join the government.

One can say that the UPA and the NDA are the functional equivalents of a two-party system. But the membership of these two alliances is fluid and the political parties are so internally divided by factions and interest groups that none is in a position to claim to assume power on its own. In many states, it is the regional parties that are stronger than the national parties. The Congress has lost its major support base in some key states. It is this development that has brought the coalition phenomenon into operation at the Centre and in several states of the Union. While none of the regional parties can hope to rule at the Centre, no national party could afford to form the government without the support of other parties, including the regional parties.

Since no political party today is in a position to form the government all by itself, attempts at forging an alliance are made soon after the election results are declared. Any alliance that succeeds in garnering more votes in the Lok Sabha puts its claim forward for running the government. A government formed by a post-election alliance cannot rightfully claim to have received its mandate from the people; and it always feels insecure lest any of its alliance partners withdraw support and join some other alliance. Such a situation of uncertainty forces the majority group within the ruling alliance to compromise with its principles, and offer concessions to its alliance partners. Leaders with doubtful credentials, even with criminal records, or known to be corrupt, get accommodated in the cabinet as ministers in the process of granting concessions.

People vote for individual party candidates or for independent candidates. They do not vote for the coalition. As such, no coalition can claim to have the mandate of the people. A hung Parliament is a consequence of a fractured mandate. A coalition is a temporal arrangement.

Changes in the Leadership

With the departure of the old leadership which was involved in the freedom struggle, and due to which it commanded respect from the masses, there is now a new leadership of mixed profile. The changing leadership profile indicates that active politicians belong to all age groups – from younger people to those who are in their late eighties; amongst the younger people who have joined politics, there are several who are children, or near relatives, of the departed leaders, or of those who are still in commanding positions. This factor is referred to as a dynastic tendency. The continuing supremacy of the Nehru-Gandhi family in the Congress party is mentioned as a glowing example of such a tendency. Other parties that are personality dominated are also seen in this light; for example, the Shiv Sena is associated with Bal Thackeray, who has anointed his son to succeed him; people also talk of the Samajwadi Party of Mulayam Singh in which his son is being groomed to take over the reins.[10]

There has also been inclusion of leaders in various parties from those who have retired from the civil service, or who have been active as lawyers. Some prominent businessmen and film stars have also joined political parties. Similarly, there is an increasing presence of women leaders.[11] With the introduction of democratic decentralization, local level leadership is getting increasingly involved in the process of governance. In Panchayati Raj institutions, the provision for women leaders had brought about a significant change in local level politics; never before so many women leaders have participated actively in the political process.

Changes in the Voter Profile

Over the years, the voter profile has changed considerably. Most of the voters today are those who were born in independent India. They did not witness British rule or the freedom struggle. They also did not see the aftermath of the partition. The younger voter is relatively better educated. The literacy rate among the female

A woman voter

voters is rising. One can say that the present day voter is much better informed and aware of his/her rights as a citizen.

In noting this change in the voter's demographic profile, it should not be forgotten that most educated voters refrain from voting. Of course, such a decision cannot always be regarded as an indicator of non-participation in politics. When people knowingly discard an election, it is also a kind of political participation. The fact that many educated people do not vote signifies the point that the parties winning the election get their mandate from the uneducated and the ill informed. And yet, it is through the ballot that power equations have kept on changing. It is important to remember this point while interpreting the mandate of the people.

Vote-Bank Politics

Analysis of election results suggests that the concept of vote-banks is a myth. The political parties constantly engage themselves in creating vote-banks on the basis of caste and religion. This is reflected in the manner in which candidates are chosen to contest elections from various constituencies, and in the way political leaders try to win the favours of the majority group. But the vote arithmetic does not work that way. It may be true that in any given constituency a particular caste or a group of castes belonging to the same status category may exhibit numerical preponderance. But when different parties nominate their candidates from the same numerically preponderant group, the consequences go counter to their strategy. These candidates divide the vote of their caste or caste cluster, and each of them is forced to gather support from other castes. In such a situation, the winner will naturally be from the same dominant group, but may come from any of the contending parties. Attributing victory to a vote-bank in such circumstances is not a valid conclusion. One should distinguish between *intention* to create a vote-bank on the basis of caste or religion and the *consequences* of such an effort. Intention is a part of the *strategy* of the political party; consequences depend on the *behaviour of the voter*. A political strategist may intend to create a vote-bank, but the voter need not oblige the party strategist. Such a distinction is generally not made in common parlance. However, it should be recognized that some personality-led political parties try to create their political bases along caste and community lines. The Bahujan Samaj Party (BSP) is one such example in which support is sought from among the Dalit groups. But even this party is now trying to change its image by seeking support from other caste groups that are regarded superior in terms of ritual hierarchy.

Role of the Judiciary

The Indian Constitution has envisaged a separation between the Executive, the Legislative, and the Judicial wings. Over the years, the Indian polity has seen increasing involvement of the judiciary in the political process. One tactic has been that of the PIL, or public interest litigation,[12] which makes it possible for a citizen to seek the intervention of the court in the public interest. This relates to corruption in public places.

The first major intervention of the court in the affairs of the Parliament was related to the election of Indira Gandhi. The court admitted the petition and declared her election void. This led to the declaration of the Emergency that suspended the entire democratic process. Several leaders of the opposition were jailed and tortured. But democracy was finally restored.

Another event was related to what is known as the Bofors deal for the purchase of guns. That matter is still sub judice.

During the NDA regime, the media exposed the corruption of some politicians and military personnel through hidden cameras that were used to record illicit transactions. This came to be known as Tehelka Kand.

This methodology of impersonation and camera recording is now used quite often to expose tainted politicians. In 2006, a media channel used this method to expose members of Parliament who were misusing the MPLAD funds.[13]

There are several cases where the role of the media and the involvement of the judiciary have been highlighted. On several constitutional matters, references have been made to the Supreme Court.

Final Comment

Given the multicultural character of the country, the Indian polity has experienced several problems that have threatened its national integration. The country's long freedom struggle to end British rule trained the leaders in organizing mass movements against the government. This included the Civil Disobedience Movement, known popularly as the Savinay Avagya Andolan. But with the attainment of independence, the leadership faced a different kind of challenge. The nationalist sentiment created during the freedom struggle had to be *institutionalized* in the political system and *internalized* in the personality systems of the citizens. This required a strategy of nation building. Such a strategy had to work simultaneously on two fronts: (i) to maintain the integrity of the country by not letting separatist tendencies grow, and (ii) to initiate a process of development – economic, social, and political.

The new political climate gave a voice to the people. Different interest groups began to articulate their demands and mobilize the masses. The country was, on the one hand, busy resettling the large number of refugees that came as a consequence of the partition; on the other, it had to respond to the demands made by people from different regions and linguistic groups. One major demand was for the reorganization of states on the basis of language. The government set up a States Reorganization Commission to attend to the demand. Associated with this was the demand for recognition of regional languages, and protests against the imposition of Hindi as a national language, instead of English. This led to many violent clashes and even some self-immolations. A three-language formula was then worked out, which retained both English and Hindi as official languages along with a regional language.

At present, the Constitution recognizes 22 languages, besides English.[14] Recent studies indicate that Hindi is the major link language and is spoken by a large number of people all over India. Since most educated persons in India are at least tri-lingual, the Hindi-speaking population is larger than those who regard it as their mother tongue. The total number of dailies published in English is 437; in Hindi, as high as 2,645. Taking all registered newspapers, weeklies, fortnightlies, monthlies, quarterlies, and annuals, the total for Hindi publications is 22,067, as against 814 in English. From these numbers one can imagine the size of the readership in Hindi and in English in India.

Regionalism took a different shape when some secessionist movements began demanding separate states. Some people in the Punjab demanded an independent Khalistan; dissident Nagas in the Northeast continue to demand a separate nationhood; the problem of Kashmir is still not settled because it has assumed an international dimension. But on all these fronts, efforts are being made to resolve the crises and ensure the integrity of the nation.

Political participation is regarded as one of the important indicators of modernization. A functioning democracy ensures people's participation in the political arena. Political parties and the entire election process have served the important function of political socialization of the masses. The fact that even with high rates of illiteracy, India has survived as a democracy shows that literacy need not be regarded as a precondition for the success of democracy. It is the democratic process that has helped improve the country's literacy profile and push its economic development. The opposition in India has a voice. The people have registered their protests through mass agitations. All strata of society, including the Dalits, have thrown up leadership at all levels. The fact of being a Dalit has not been an obstacle for a qualified person to occupy the highest office of the State. The country has had Presidents who came from the minorities – Sikh and Muslim – or from a Dalit group. The national leadership represents the entire spectrum of Indian society.

There is a definite march towards an egalitarian society. No doubt riots occur, communities clash, fundamentalist voices are raised, but these do not outdo the record of peaceful co-existence.

India is managing its multiplicity quite well.

Notes

1. Paul R. Brass, *The Politics of India Since Independence*, 1997, 2nd edition reprint, Foundation Books, Delhi, p.1.
2. For communalism, see Harish Sharma, *Communal Angle in Indian Politics,* 2000, Rawat Publications, Jaipur.
3. This is not a new feature. Way back in 1971, I analysed the manifestoes of various parties and published an article in *The Hindustan Times* of 26 March 1971. In an article published in *The Hindustan Times* of 31 March 1998, C.P. Bhambhri called the Congress a 'party without ideology'. In the special supplement of *The Tribune*, on the occasion of its 125th anniversary, Pratap Bhanu Mehta wrote: "The paradox is that the number of political parties has no bearing on the diversities of views represented... The ideological differences between most parties are minimal..."
4. There have been 92 Amendments to the Constitution of India (See *India 2005*, Publications Division, Government of India).
5. The reader should note that the Brahmans are not a caste, but a caste cluster, or a *varna*. However, such fine distinctions are forgotten in politics.
6. See 'Fetish of Secularism' in Yogesh Atal's *Mandate for Political Transition,* 2000, Rawat Publications, Jaipur, pp. 260-3.
7. Paul Brass, ibid., p. 19.
8. Maharana Bhopal Singhji.
9. See Rajni Kothari, *Party System and Election Studies*, 1967, Allied Publishers, New Delhi, p. 2.
10. Some oft-quoted names are those of Jyotiraditya Scindia (son of the late Madhav Rao Scindia of Gwalior), Sachin Pilot (son of the late Rajesh Pilot), and Omar Abdullah (son of Farooq Abdullah and grandson of Sheikh Abdullah).
11. One can easily name Sonia Gandhi, Ambika Soni, Sushma Swaraj, Uma Bharati, Mamta Banerjee, Brinda Karat, Jaya Jaitley, Vasundhara Raje, and J. Jayalalithaa.
12. This was introduced in 1985 during the tenure of Justice P.N. Bhagwati.

13. MPLAD stands for Member of Parliament Local Area Development Fund. Each MP receives an annual fund of Rs 2 crore to be disbursed in his/her constituency for developmental projects.
14. These languages are Assamese, Bengali, Bodo, Dogri, Gujarati, Hindi, Kannada, Kashmiri, Konkani, Maithili, Malayalam, Manipuri, Marathi, Nepali, Oriya, Punjabi, Sanskrit, Santhali, Sindhi, Tamil, Telugu, and Urdu.

10

Changing India

In this chapter . . .

Change is a characteristic of all societies – be they primitive or modern. No society ever remains changeless. It is a different matter whether societies change slowly or experience revolutionary changes. A society going through revolutionary changes may lose its earlier identity because of the replacement of a large number of structures. Its merger with another society may make it a subsystem.

A society may perish due to some catastrophe. Prehistoric investigations have brought to the surface evidence of several such human societies that flourished in the past, but have now become extinct. In India, we have instances of Mohen-jo-daro and Harappa, cultures which once flourished, but are now extinct. At times, the inhabitants of a given settlement may abandon it altogether for one reason or the other and settle elsewhere. In due course of time, such settlements are covered by sand and become mounds. They may be discovered later. But that will be an example of a dead society.

To an extent, a living human society can be compared with an organism. Like an organism, a society also grows. In the process, it begins to look different, but its identity is not lost. A society either enlarges or gets smaller, changes its demographic contours, or even its geographic boundaries, but these changes do not alter its identity. A living society continually changes in response to developments in the natural and social environment, and also through the behaviour of its members.

When foreigners described India as a 'traditional' society, they implied that it was a society that stuck to its traditions and refused to change. But this is only a partial truth. Resisting a particular change, which has been brought about from the outside, does not mean that a society refuses to change. All societies have their cultural monitors to screen all entries and take adequate measures to receive or reject them. Similarly, all societies put restrictions at their exit points, to allow or retain departures. These are called a society's apertures and insulators. Any living culture has a mix of tradition and modernity. Tradition represents continuity; modernity designates change, or recency of arrival. In the midst of the rapid changes brought about by revolution in information technology and the growing globalization, enormous social transformation is occurring in all societies. India is no exception.

When India became independent, it became a union with the merger of several princely states that had a special relationship with British India, but it also lost some of its territory and a sizeable population. Both the geographical boundaries and the demographic contours of India were radically affected by the fact of partition. Independent India also saw the reorganization of the states, incorporation of the Portuguese ruled Goa, Diu, and Daman, and the joining of Sikkim through a referendum. The resettlement of the refugees that came from the then Western and Eastern wings of Pakistan changed the demography and affected the economy of the places where they were rehabilitated. The Sindhi population, which came from West Pakistan lost its land, but preserved its culture and language. These people now mainly inhabit places in Rajasthan, Gujarat, and Maharashtra. Sindhi is accorded the status of a recognised language in the Indian Constitution. The geographical province of Sindh is in Pakistan, but the Sindhi subculture is alive and flourishing amongst the erstwhile migrants and their descendents settled in the places where they were relocated. Of course, interactions with local cultures have changed their profiles into new 'sandwich cultures'.[1]

Let us briefly summarize the changes that have occurred in India's social structure and culture.

Changes in Demography

Demography tells the story of the process of recruitment of a society's members. At any given point of time, the size of a population is determined by the birth of new members, the death of existing members, and by the processes of immigration and emigration.

In terms of absolute numbers, India's population has grown enormously in the last hundred years covering the period from 1901 through 2001. From 238 million in 1901 India's population has gone up to 1.02 billion in 2001, registering an increase of 331.47 per cent in 100 years. Between 1951 (when the first Census in Independent India was undertaken) and 2001 (the last Census year), the population has grown from 371 million to 1,027 million. There are estimates that by 2050, India might surpass China in population size and become the most populated country in the world. The increase in population has occurred despite efforts at family planning. It is the decline in death rate that has contributed to the continuing rise in numbers.[2] As of today, our growth rate is 1.8 per cent per annum. Even if this comes down further, the absolute numbers are going to be enormous. India has to continually adapt to the phenomenon of population explosion. The infrastructure that existed in the 1950s had to expand to fulfil the basic needs of the ever-rising population. Education, health, sanitation, drinking water, housing, roads, communication, jobs – almost everything – has been affected by the population explosion. Infrastructure for all these areas has been considerably expanded, and yet there have been shortfalls. The mismatch between demand and supply continues to pose problems. Defects in manpower planning resulted in oversupply of certain skills and dearth of others. The growing unemployment and continuing high rates of poverty are regarded as direct consequences of unmanaged population growth.

What has been worrying is the fact that with the growth of the population, there has been a decline in sex ratio.[3] From 951 in 1951, it went down to 927 in 1991, and has shown a little rise in 2001 to 933. The sex ratio is worse in Northern and Western India than in Southern and Eastern India. These imbalances are due to several factors, including migration of males in search of livelihoods, preference for smaller families, and, most importantly, female foeticide, exhibiting a gender bias.

Demographic changes are also to be seen in the age pyramid. According to the 2001 Census, 34.8 per cent of the country's population is below 14 years of age. Those between 15 and 59 years constitute 58.1 per cent, and the older people constitute 7 per cent. It is significant to note that the number of the aged is going to increase in the coming years because of increasing longevity. From 5.6 per cent in 1951, this percentage has gone up to 7 in 2001. By 2025, the aged are likely to constitute 12.5 per cent of the population; by 2050, they would claim 20.6 per cent of the total population.

Prolonged life expectancy is not only a demographic fact; it also has immense sociological implications. In the years to come, society will have to develop programmes for the care of the large number of aged people. Expenses on pension and medical care are likely to increase. Hospitals will have to develop specializations for gerontological cases; families will have to devote more time, and for a longer number of years, to look after aged family members; community services for the aged will have to be provided, and efforts will be needed to utilize the services and skills of the elder members (retirees) of society.[4]

Changes in the Family

All these demographic changes have affected the Indian family. Several studies have shown that the Joint family is the idealized pattern, but was never a noticeable phenomenon in reality. Every family experiences in its life cycle a period when more than two generations, or siblings with their spouses and children, live together; but it is a temporal phase. With the rising rates of mobilization, extended families are getting separated physically. Thus, while family ties continue, the fact of co-residence is getting confined more and more to nuclear families. The NRI phenomenon has further encouraged such separation. Successful sons or daughters residing abroad do maintain their ties with parents and in-laws, and even support them financially, but they remain away for longer durations. Once a year, particularly during the summers, children settled abroad invite their parents or in-laws to spend some time with them, or they visit them in India. That is a period of family reunion. But because of this distance, the hierarchy of control within the family has been somewhat diluted. The NRI phenomenon has made many middle class families richer and upwardly mobile. While NRIs live abroad in distinct sandwich cultures, their families of orientation back home move to reside in better locations and adopt a different lifestyle, which includes occasional international travel.

Some other changes in marriage and family may also be noted:

1. There have been changes in the age for marriage, coupled with rise in literacy rates. Because of late marriages, women stay longer with their parents and continue their studies to brighten the prospects of their marriage. Some join the labour force. In metropolitan centres, several jobs have been created by the corporate sector, particularly the BPOs[5], popularly known as call centres; many young girls work in them to earn handsome salaries. These centres also provide greater freedom to them to be in the company of persons of the opposite sex. This change has affected many behaviour patterns associated with marriage and family. One does not know the extent of premarital mating, but it is generally believed that it is on the rise. A remark in support of such behaviour by a famous film star from South India created a stir and generated a countrywide debate. Alongside of the rising age for marriage amongst the urban educated, child marriages are still common in the villages and small towns.

2. There has been broadening of the endogamous frontier, and greater frequency of inter-caste and inter-religious marriages. Two other features are significant: (i) search for spouses through the mass media (newspaper advertisements), and (ii) love marriages (which, in many cases, get formalized with the consent of the parents of the two parties and become instances of inter-caste marriages. This is, however, not to deny the fact that love marriages do occur within the caste as well, and in such cases, some traditionally tabooed relationships are ignored.
3. There has been a remarkable reduction in marriage rituals, including the period of celebration, but there is also a noticeable rise in conspicuous consumption. Lavish dinners and grand decorations at farmhouses, video filming of the celebrations and grand gifts are becoming the order of the day. Demands for dowry are on the rise and the inventory of things being given in dowry has been constantly changing. It is also important to note that now even daughters prod their parents to spend more on their weddings and to give them a large dowry. While the family of the bridegroom is usually blamed for the menace of dowry, the fact of daughters making excessive demands on their parents is generally overlooked.
4. The new trends have also created newer types of family crises. For example, dowry deaths, the bride refusing to marry when excess demands are made for dowry, and even reporting such cases to the police, marriage delays, indebtedness, suicides, divorces, domestic violence, and, at times, communal riots to protest against inter-religious love marriages.
5. Changes are being seen in fertility behaviour and in family planning practices. The continuing preference for male children has led to malpractices in the medical profession. Private clinics clandestinely conduct

sonographic tests for sex determination of the embryo; as a consequence, there is a rise in the number of doctor-assisted abortion cases. Female foeticide is a most worrying phenomenon.

6. The fact of women entering the world of work has affected the family time-table and role responsibilities. It is also affecting child socialization – domestic servants and nursery schools perform the role of surrogate mothers.

Urbanization and Industrialization

Measured in terms of the number of people living in urban areas, urbanization has shown a phenomenal rise in India. From 26 million in 1901, the urban population today stands at 285 million. But it still constitutes only 27.8 per cent of the total population. This implies that the country is still rural with 72.2 per cent of its people living in villages. The current decadal growth rate is 36.4 per cent.

While there are 3,609 urban settlements in India, rural settlements number 5,80,781[6], ranging from those that have a population of over 10,000 persons to those with even less than 500 people. Over the years, many large villages and towns have expanded and become more urban. Some villages have got absorbed into the expanding cities. The arrival of urban amenities in several villages has changed their profile. Many villages now have electricity – and, therefore, radio and TV – and better quality link roads. As a result, rural-urban interactions have increased.

Urbanization is closely associated with industrialization. After liberalization, Indian economy is fast expanding. With the introduction of the new industrial policy in 1991, there has been substantial deregulation. As a result, many industries have been set up. Even those industries that were earlier reserved for the public sector have been opened up. The defence industry has been

Changing face of urban India

opened up to the private sector, with foreign direct investment (FDI) of up to 26 per cent. As a result, there has been a dramatic increase in production. For example, cement production has gone up from 623 tonnes in 1994-95 to 1,234 tonnes in 2003-04; fertilizers, from 104.38 tonnes to 142 tonnes; and coal from 2,537.3 tonnes to 3,557.2 tonnes. The vehicle industry has shown robust growth. The sale of passenger cars, multi-utility vehicles, commercial vehicles, and two and three wheelers has increased from 41,15,894 in 1998-99 to 67,94,812 in 2003-04. The ever-increasing number of vehicles on the road has affected the infrastructure of the settlements, has contributed to traffic jams and road accidents, and increased expenditure on gasoline. It has also affected the lifestyle of the people.

The last few decades have also seen growth of agro and rural industries. This has brought benefits to the rural non-farm sector and the overall growth of the national economy. Banking has also extended to the villages. Rural life today is becoming different from what it was in the 1950s as a consequence of urbanization, industrialization, and the spread of literacy.

Changing Literacy Profile

While India is still struggling to eradicate illiteracy, it is heartening to note that our literacy rate has gone up from 25 per cent in 1951 to 64.8 per cent in 2001. It is true that this percentage includes everyone who knows how to read and write a few alphabets, and may not be considered a true indicator of education; however, the rise in the percentage is quite noticeable. It indicates how much still remains to be done to achieve 100 per cent literacy. It also shows the magnitude of demand that is likely to be made on the education system for higher learning. Infrastructure will have to be expanded to accommodate the burgeoning number of students seeking admission to secondary, higher secondary, and tertiary education. The classrooms, teachers, libraries and laboratory facilities, hostels, and playfields needed for the rising number of student clientele will have to be provided. Already we know that the existing system is unable to meet the rising demand. As a consequence, many surrogate institutions have sprung up outside of the education system to train aspiring students. Coaching centres, tuition classes, 'institutes' and 'universities' have been set up in the private sector, not all of which are of acceptable standards. Such institutions have commercialized education and put it beyond the reach of the poor and the deprived.

A continuing worry is the lower rate of literacy among women. Sixty per cent of the non-literates in India are women, although the female literacy rate has gone up from 9 per cent in the 1950s to 54 per cent in 2001. But the gender gap in literacy is enormous; the difference between the male and female literacy rate is 22 percentage points – that is, there are more male literates than female. Some states and some areas within the states have shown higher rates of illiteracy among women, and efforts are afoot to improve the situation through the Sarva Shiksha Abhiyan of the government of India.

As is expected, the literacy rate in the urban areas is higher than in the rural. Table 1 illustrates this.

Table 1

Literacy Rate in India: Rural-Urban and Male-Female

Year	*Male*	*Female*	*Overall*
1981			
Rural	49.7	21.8	36.1
Urban	76.8	56.4	67.3
Total	56.5	29.9	43.7
1991			
Rural	57.9	30.6	44.7
Urban	81.1	64.1	73.1
Total	64.1	39.3	52.2
2001			
Rural	71.2	46.6	59.2
Urban	86.4	73.0	80.1
Total	75.9	54.2	65.4

It is clear that change has occurred in the literacy profile on both variables, namely gender and settlement, and the change is for the better. Because of the changes in literacy, one can expect changes in other aspects of the life of the people in terms of job opportunities, marriage, and mobility. It might also bring about changes in interpersonal and inter-group relations.

Changing Profile of Communication

During the 50 years of its independence, India has made significant strides in the area of transportation and communication. These networks serve the function of integration as they enhance both physical and psychological mobility of the people, and thus pave the way for their social mobility.

Transport

India had its first railway line of 34 kilometres in 1852. In 1947, when India became free, the country had 54,814 km of railway lines. In 2003, it increased to 63,140 km. However, the total running track is 82,492 km.

The country had 397,619 km of roads in 1950-51, by 1961, this had nearly doubled to 705,002 km of roads. Today, India has one of the largest road networks, totalling 3.32 million kilometres. Of these, the national highways and state highways together account for 1,95,000 km in length. The government of India has embarked upon a massive National Highways Development Project (NHDP). As part of this project, 14,279 km of national highways are to be upgraded to four or six lanes. The Golden Quadrilateral (GQ), which will connect the four metro cities – Delhi, Mumbai, Chennai, and Kolkata – will cover 5,846 km; the North-South and East-West Corridors – connecting Srinagar to Kanyakumari and Silchar to Porbandar, respectively – will cover 7,300 km. Roads are also being developed in the rural areas under the Pradhan Mantri Gram Sadak Yojana (PMGSY). Under this scheme, all villages with a population of more than 500 will be linked with all-weather roads by 2007. This huge programme of road construction will greatly increase connectivity between rural and urban centres and between states. Already, people have begun using road transport for long journeys because of better roads and good quality motor vehicles; this has somewhat lessened the burden on the railways.

A significant development has been in the area of civil aviation. In addition to the newly renamed Indian and its subsidiary, Alliance Air, private scheduled airlines and air taxis provide domestic services. Even in international air services, Air-India is joined by two private airlines. There has been enormous change in the area of civil aviation. Not only are more people opting to travel by air within the country to a number of places that were earlier not served, but the number of people going abroad is also increasing manifold.

Mass Media and Communication

Exposure to mass media has greatly increased over the years. There are more people now exposed to the mass media. The interesting point is that while newspapers and magazines are restricted to the literate and educated population, the electronic media have made the requirement of literacy almost redundant. Visual images and audio messages create a powerful impact over the masses. The epics of the *Mahabharat* and *Ramayana,* serialized through the television for months together, attracted large audiences and influenced their behaviour pattern. Several of the chaste Hindi phrases and modes of address became part of the popular parlance. People's dresses were also affected by them. With the arrival of private channels and satellite technology, the Indian viewer is now exposed to a wide variety of programmes.

It must be noted that television is a recent arrival in the country. From a few stations in the early 1970s, television is now becoming universal. If, in the 1960s, transistor sets brought about a revolution, the 1970s saw the beginnings of the TV era. From black and white TV to colour TV, and then to cable TV has been a fast journey. With this, the government monopoly over the media has also gone. Now the Indian viewer is exposed to a wide variety of TV channels – regional, national, and international. Through them, the viewer is exposed to a wide range of programmes,

Growing media culture

thereby becoming the decision maker of what he/she wants to see. Round-the-clock news channels have somewhat stolen the importance of newspapers.

Census 2001 suggests that 64.3 per cent of urban households and 18.9 per cent of rural households now own TV sets. Since ownership of a TV set requires expenditure on purchase of the TV set, access to electricity, and cost of a cable connection, it is a good indicator of affluence. It also suggests greater exposure to the wider world than the community of one's residence.

With the rise in literacy rates, there is also an expected rise in the circulation of newspapers. See the Table 2.

In the 1950s, it was conventional to examine the statistics relative to telephones because it was available to a very limited number of people. In the metropolitan centres, there used to be 10-year-long waiting lists for acquiring a telephone connection. Today, telephones are getting somewhat outdated with the arrival of cell phones. The history of cellular phones is very recent. In

Table 2
Total Circulation of Newspapers in India

Language	*Total Circulation*	*Distribution (%)*
English	7,851,426	13.3
Hindi	25,577,406	43.2
Others	25,700,351	43.5
Total	59,129,183	100.0

Source: Ministry of Information & Broadcasting, 2001

1994, cellular licences were first awarded to private operators in metropolitan cities. By September 2002, this service was available in over 1,500 cities and towns. From 3.4 million cell phones in use in the country in 1997, the number has gone up to 127 million in 2003. And the number is rising day by day. A cell phone is becoming almost a necessity, rather than a status symbol. Not only high-profile officials and businessmen, even petty domestic servants own cell phones today. They have greatly enhanced connectivity and reduced distances. They are also put to multiple uses, including the Internet. In feature films and serials, their use can be seen regularly. Thus, they have influenced literature and performing arts; they have also become part of the underworld culture. Children have acquired new freedom to converse with their friends and lovers, disregarding the control of their parents. SMS and MMS have become new modes of communication. unfortunately, they are also being used for anti-social activities and as pornographic tools.

Changes in Political Culture

Indian democracy has matured over the years. Some major changes that have occurred in the polity may be briefly summarized here:

1. Enlarging party structure and the emerging phenomenon of coalition governments;
2. Increasing involvement of leaders from the Dalit and backward groups, including their participation in government, both in the states and at the Centre. Similarly, female participation in politics is on the rise. In Panchayats, their participation has increased quite a bit. Efforts are also being made to ensure their greater participation in Parliament and state assemblies through an acceptable formula for reservation of seats;
3. Increasing role of the civil society. Several NGOs have been set up and they mobilize people and help them articulate their demands. The Right to Information Act has come into force through their active campaigns. NGOs have also been responsible for the rising number of public interest litigations (PILs) in the Supreme Court;
4. Mass media have played a significant role in the political socialization of the masses. They have also exposed corrupt officials and politicians, including ministers, through sting operations. These operations have reinforced the people's sense of political efficacy;
5. There has been communalization of politics and politicization of caste and communities. These developments have given a fresh impetus to the debate regarding secularism;
6. With liberalization policies and privatization, the state hold over the economy has changed somewhat. Indian politics and governance are influenced in several ways by multinationals and big business houses, and
7. Voting participation amongst the intelligentsia remains indifferent. Voting percentage is regarded as a mandate of the people, but deeper analysis suggests that it leads

to over-generalization. However, recent election results have exploded the myth of bulk voting, based on the principle of vote-banks. The Indian voter is becoming shrewd enough to falsify the vote-bank strategy.

Changes in Caste

The caste system as it exists today is vastly different from the descriptions that are found in earlier literature on the caste system authored by Indologists, and even foreign writers. The present-day caste is vastly different from the attributions of Manu. These changes are striking in the context of cities and urban conglomerates. Interactions with people in these centres are not guided by caste considerations. When migration occurs from rural areas and from distant states, the caste of the migrants cannot be ascertained. People hiring them for work – generally for domestic help, or as construction workers, carpenters, electricians, etc. – seldom bother about their caste status. Anonymity allows ambiguity to prevail. Thus, there exists a dual morality. In the villages – particularly those that are less exposed to the trends of modernity – the caste system may still be intact in terms of caste-based occupations and commensal relations, put in the cities, caste norms are greatly relaxed. Who bothers, for example, to know the caste of the cooks or waiters in a restaurant?

The caste system – that is the relationship between castes in a given setting – has been seriously affected in the sense that interactions have been released from the restrictions imposed by the caste ideology of hierarchy based on concepts of purity and pollution. Castes as units have, however, not disappeared. People do use a caste referent as part of their individual names – the last name denotes either the name of the caste, or *gotra*, or *varna*. The preference for marriage within the caste reigns supreme, but there has been change on the endogamous frontier. Marriages are being held outside of the subcultural region, but within the same caste.

Minor differences of sub-castes are being ignored and marriages are permitted in a broader caste cluster or in a *varna* category. Thus, a Brahman marrying a Brahman may mean: (i) marriage within the same caste or (ii) marriage between people of two castes within the Brahman *varna*. Instances are also found of some restrictions of exogamy being relaxed and marriages being allowed among closer kin – that is tertiary and quaternary relatives.

The most important change is to be seen in terms of the continuing decline in the relationship between caste and occupation. It is true that while some people engage themselves in caste-related occupations, several others opt for other open occupations. Some caste-based occupations that are not defiling are also taken over by people of other castes. Overall, caste restrictions, both at the level of the unit and the system, are being relaxed. It is striking that while socially, caste is losing its significance, politically, group solidarity at the level of caste, or caste cluster, is being reinforced by the political parties with a view to creating their respective vote-banks.

Final Comment

Indian social life is changing on all fronts. All our settlements, particularly urban – and, in the future, more urbanization is likely to occur – are becoming pluricultural and multi-religious. With migration and plurality of ethnic and religious groups, India faces the continuing challenge of managing multiplicity. This multiplicity makes individual citizens bearers of multiple roles, which make them simultaneously both insiders and outsiders in different social contexts.[7] For developing an integrated nation, this multiplicity is an asset. What is needed is to ensure that groups do not get insulated from each other and channels of communication remain open for them to interact and empathize with each other.

Waves of modernization and globalization are reaching all corners of society, breaking their insulation and opening out apertures. These have affected local cultures and social structures in meaningful ways to adapt to the changing environs.

Notes

1. I have coined the term, *Sandhivichi Sanskriti,* in Hindi for the concept of sandwich culture.
2. Our birth rate has come down from 37.2 per 1,000 in the 1970s to 25.8 per 1,000 in the 1990s. But the death rate has also come down from 15 per 1,000 to 8.5 per 1,000 during the same period.
3. It is the number of females per 1,000 males.
4. For details, see Desai, Murli, and S. Siva Raju (eds), *Ageing in India, Gerontological Social Work in India,* 2000, B.R. Publishing Corporation, Delhi. Read S. Siva Raju's essay, pp. 27-58.
5. BPO stands for business process outsourcing.
6. *India 2005* gives the figure of 593,643, p. 17.
7. See my article, 'Managing Multiplicity: The Insider-Outsider Duality', *Economic and Political Weekly,* Vol. XXXVI, No. 36, 8 September 2001, pp. 3459-3466. Reprinted in *Social Exclusion*: *Essays in Honour of Dr Bindeshwar Pathak,* edited by A.K. Lal, 2003, Volume I, Concept Publishing Company, New Delhi.

Select Readings

Atal, Yogesh (ed.), *Understanding Indian Society,* 1992, Har Anand Publications, New Delhi.

Atal, Yogesh, *Mandate for Political Transition*, 2000, Rawat Publications, Jaipur.

Atal, Yogesh, *The Changing Frontiers of Caste*, 1979, Second edition, National Publishing House, Delhi.

Brass, Paul R., *The Politics of India Since Independence*, 1997, 2nd edition reprint, Foundation Books, Delhi.

Breese, Gerald, *Urbanization in Newly Developing Countries,* 1969, Prentice-Hall of India Private Limited, New Delhi.

Chauhan, Brij Raj, *India: A Socio-Economic Profile*, 1989, AASSREC and Sterling Publishers Pvt. Ltd., New Delhi.

Cohn, Bernard S., *India: The Social Anthropology of a Civilization,* 2000, Oxford University Press, New Delhi.

Desai, A.R. (ed.), *Rural Sociology in India 1969*, 4th Revised Edition, Popular Prakashan, Mumbai.

Dube, S.C. *Indian Village*, 1955, Routledge and Kegan Paul, London (Its Hindi translation by Yogesh Atal, titled *Ek Bharatiya Gram,* is published by Vani Prakashan, Delhi in 1996).

Dube, S.C., *Indian Society 1990,* National Book Trust, New Delhi.

Jalan, Bimal, *The Future of India: Politics, Economics, and Governance*, 2005, Viking/Pelican, New Delhi.

Khilnani, Sunil, *The Idea of India*, 1995, Penguin Books India, New Delhi.

Kothari, Rajni, *Politics in India,* 1970, Orient Longman, New Delhi.

Liebig, Phoebe S. and S. Irudaya Rajan (ed.), *An Aging India: Perspectives, Prospects, and Policies,* 2003. The Haworth Press, Binghamonton, N.Y.

Mandelbaum, David G. (ed.), *Society in India,* 1972, Popular Prakashan, Mumbai.

Marriott, Mckim (ed.), *Village India*, 1955, University of Chicago.

Nayar, Sushila, and Kamla Mankekar (eds.), *Women Pioneers in India's Renaissance, 2002,* National Book Trust, New Delhi.

Publications Division, *India 2005,* Ministry of Information and Broadcasting, Government of India.

Sen, Gertrude Emerson, *Cultural Unity of India, 1969,* Publication Division, Ministry of Information and Broadcasting, Government of India, New Delhi.

Shah, A.M., *The Family in India: Critical Essays*, 1998, Orient Longman, Hyderabad.

Sharma, Harish, *Communal Angle in Indian Politics, 2000,* Rawat Publications, Jaipur.

Srinivas, M.N., *Social Change in Modern India,* Reprinted in 2002, Orient Longman Pvt. Ltd., New Delhi.

Sunil Kumar, *Communalism and Secularism in Indian Politics,* 2001, Rawat Publications, Jaipur.

Index